A WAY OF READING JOHN'S GOSPEL

A WAY *of* READING JOHN'S GOSPEL

Cruciform Structures in a Cruciform Gospel

GRAEME FINLAY

WIPF & STOCK · Eugene, Oregon

A WAY OF READING JOHN'S GOSPEL
Cruciform Structures in a Cruciform Gospel

Copyright © 2024 Graeme Finlay. All rights reserved. Except for brief quotations in critical publications or reviews, no part of this book may be reproduced in any manner without prior written permission from the publisher. Write: Permissions, Wipf and Stock Publishers, 199 W. 8th Ave., Suite 3, Eugene, OR 97401.

Wipf & Stock
An Imprint of Wipf and Stock Publishers
199 W. 8th Ave., Suite 3
Eugene, OR 97401

www.wipfandstock.com

PAPERBACK ISBN: 979-8-3852-2259-9
HARDCOVER ISBN: 979-8-3852-2260-5
EBOOK ISBN: 979-8-3852-2261-2

VERSION NUMBER 11/19/24

Scripture translations have been taken from Good News Translation® (Today's English Version, Second Edition) © 1992 American Bible Society. All rights reserved.

Scripture translations have been taken from The Jerusalem Bible, published and copyright 1966,1967 and 1968 by Darton, Longman & Todd Ltd and Doubleday and Co. Inc.

Scripture translations have been taken from The New Testament in Modern English by J. B. Phillips copyright © 1960, 1972 J. B. Phillips. Administered by The Archbishops' Council of the Church of England.

Scripture translations have been taken from Holy Bible, New International Version®, NIV® Copyright ©1973, 1978, 1984, 2011 by Biblica, Inc.® All rights reserved worldwide.

Scripture translations have been taken from Revised Standard Version of the Bible, copyright © 1946, 1952, and 1971 the Division of Christian Education of the National Council of the Churches of Christ in the United States of America. All rights reserved.

With thanks to God for Jean
wife, friend, lover, fellow pilgrim for forty years

Dear Jean has gone *from* me—inexpressible pain;
she's gone *to* God's own place—incomparable gain.
She has gone *from* us—our hearts ache beyond telling
but wonder! She's gone *to* the Father's glad dwelling.
She's gone *from* our space-time—her loss leaves us weeping
but gone *to* the sheepfold for the Shepherd's safe keeping.
She once described joy as being spiritual pleasure;
here it is partial but there hers beyond measure.
Rapt with the Son's sacrifice she sings to his praise
his resurrection, now hers, the goal of her days.
Jean and I alike abide close to God's loving heart;
in union with the triune God we are not far apart.

CONTENTS

List of Figures | ix
List of Tables | xii
Preface | xiii
Abbreviations | xvii

1. Introduction: The Gospel of John | 1
2. Patterns in the Text | 5
3. John 1: Divine Word and Human Witness | 16
4. John 2: Transformation of the Old Age to the New Age | 26
5. John 3: Spiritual Birth to Eternal Life | 32
6. John 4: Life-Giving Spirit, Life-Giving Son | 40
7. John 5: Lord of the Sabbath I: Opposing Spiritual Deadness | 47
8. John 6: Bread That Gives Life | 53
9. John 7–8: Festival of Shelters Disputation | 61
10. John 9: Lord of the Sabbath II: Opposing Spiritual Blindness | 70
11. John 10: Jesus Is the Good Shepherd | 74
12. John 11: Jesus Is the Resurrection | 81
13. John 12: Worship of Mary and Farewell to the Crowds | 85
14. John 13–17: Farewell to the Disciples | 92
15. John 18–19: Arrest, Trials, and Crucifixion | 120
16. John 20: Resurrection and Divine Vindication | 131
17. John 21: Commissioning of Peter and the Beloved Disciple | 139

Bibliography | 145
Index | 149

LIST OF FIGURES

Figure 1. Paul's Sorrow, Triumph, and Work | 7

Figure 2. Jews and Gentiles Are Saved on the Same Basis | 8

Figure 3. Prologue: From God's Son (the Divine Word) to God's Children | 17

Figure 4. The Declaration of John the Baptist | 20

Figure 5. The Calling of the First Disciples | 23

Figure 6. The Wedding Feast: From the Water of Ritual to the Wine of Celebration (Sign 1) | 28

Figure 7. Passover: Transitioning from the Old to the New Exodus (Defining the Future, Sign 7) | 30

Figure 8. Entry into God's Kingdom Requires Both Physical and Spiritual Birth | 34

Figure 9. Receiving Eternal Life Requires that People Believe in the Son | 36

Figure 10. John the Baptist Is Farewelled; Jesus' Supremacy Is Affirmed | 38

Figure 11. Jesus Gives Life-Giving Water | 41

Figure 12. Jesus Inaugurates the True Worship, Enabled by God's Spirit | 42

Figure 13. Jesus' Power over Life and Death: The Boy at Capernaum (Sign 2) | 45

List of Figures

Figure 14. Sabbath Healing at Bethzatha (Sign 3) | 48

Figure 15. Sabbath Healing: United Work of Father and Son | 49

Figure 16. Sabbath Healing: Heed the Witnesses | 51

Figure 17. Jesus Feeds a Large Crowd with Five Loaves and Two Fish (Sign 4, the Central One) | 54

Figure 18. Jesus Rules Creation | 56

Figure 19. Jesus Is the Life-Giving Bread That Came from Heaven | 57

Figure 20. The Life-Giving Father, Son, and Spirit | 60

Figure 21. Controversy at the Festival of Shelters: Who Is This Man? | 63

Figure 22. Jesus Challenges an Adulterous Woman and Self-Righteous Men | 68

Figure 23. Sabbath Healing at Siloam (Sign 5) | 71

Figure 24. The Metaphor of the Sheep and the Shepherd | 75

Figure 25. Jesus Teaches: Festival of the Dedication of the Temple | 78

Figure 26. Raising of Lazarus (Sign 6) | 83

Figure 27. Mary and Judas at the Hinge of History | 86

Figure 28. Return of the King | 87

Figure 29. Last Appeal to the People | 89

Figure 30. Concluding Summary of Jesus' Mission | 91

Figure 31. Jesus Serves | 94

Figure 32. Betrayal to Glory | 96

Figure 33. The Love of the Triune God | 98

Figure 34. Unity with Jesus the Vine | 104

Figure 35. Hatred of the World | 106

Figure 36. Sadness to Gladness | 109

Figure 37. Jesus' Prayer | 113

List of Figures

Figure 38. Jesus' Prayer Regarding the Father and Himself | 116

Figure 39. Jesus' Prayer for the Disciples Then Present | 117

Figure 40. Jesus' Prayer for All Disciples Who Were Still Future | 118

Figure 41. Arrest of Jesus | 121

Figure 42. Trial in Annas's House: Who Is the Real High Priest? | 123

Figure 43. Trial Before Prefect Pilate: Who Is the Real King? | 125

Figure 44. Crucifixion (First Phase of Sign 7) | 128

Figure 45. Mary Discovers the Empty Tomb (Second Phase of Sign 7) | 132

Figure 46. Jesus Appears to Mary of Magdala | 134

Figure 47. Particularity of History: Disciples *See* and Express *Joy* | 135

Figure 48. Universality of Gospel: All Who *Believe* in Jesus' Deity Are *Blessed* | 136

Figure 49. Breakfast on the Beach: "It Is the Lord!" | 140

Figure 50. The Ideal Witness Signs Off | 142

LIST OF TABLES

Table 1. Transformation of the Old Creation to the New (Signs 1, 7) | 10

Table 2. Jesus' Authority over Life and Death (Signs 2, 6) | 11

Table 3. Jesus Highlights Spiritual Blindness (Signs 3, 5) | 11

Table 4. A Possible Chiastic Structure of the Farewell Discourse | 93

PREFACE

FOR MANY PEOPLE, JOHN'S Gospel is a particularly loved part of the Bible. People are attracted to, and challenged by, its portrayal of Jesus and its accounts of Jesus' teachings and of his dialogues with disciples and critics. In my own reading of John, I have always been struck by the wealth of the ideas expressed, but in this richness, I have also struggled to perceive the ways in which the themes undergo development. Part of this complexity is that the text has often seemed repetitious.

As a lay preacher I have, over the years, been given the privilege of presenting talks on John's Gospel. As I have pored over the text, I have come to realize that, in many cases, sections of the Gospel are arranged in a chiastic pattern. This is a typically Jewish way of writing. A sequence of ideas is presented (let's symbolize four such ideas by the alphabetic letters ABCD) and then they are repeated, but in reverse order. The unit of text would then read according to a mirror image pattern (A-B-C-D-D'-C'-B'-A'). The *prime* symbol (the little dash, ') identifies the second element of a pair. The pairing of elements accounts for the apparent repetitiousness of John's Gospel. The second element of a pair may emphasize, expand upon, or provide new perspectives on what was stated in the first. The central elements (D and D' in this scheme) may contain a particularly important thought.

This approach seems to provide a way of identifying the natural units of John's Gospel (chapter boundaries in our Bibles are not always well placed). It brings order and unity to a passage of text of

Preface

which scholars may have postulated complicated histories.[1] Being aware of chiastic structures may thus simplify analysis of a section of text. It may help the reader to identify the most important motifs. And it may emphasize the impact of the centrally placed element(s).

Some candidate chiastic units seem to be very clear and convincing. Others were more subtle. Perhaps some chiasms merely followed the way dramatic engagements unfold, with an ascent to a climax, the key point or punch line at the centre, and then the descent from that climax as the drama resolves. Other chiasms may arise because many themes are intermingled and abundantly reiterated, so that *selective* abstraction of certain repeated ideas could give a spurious perception of chiastic structure. We might need a statistician to show how often a selection of randomly repeated ideas might be able to provide a chiastic pattern. Nevertheless, I offer those I have identified, so readers can assess them for themselves and decide whether they provide any help in the way the text of John is read.[2]

I have had a career in biomedical science. When I was a student, a lab partner said to me, "Finlay, you can rationalize anything!" If people who read this book are not convinced by the schemes presented, I will be well content that they have engaged deeply with the narrative and text of John's Gospel. To engage with John is to be enriched.

I have at times brought a scientific mindset to my approach to John's Gospel. For example, when I failed to find chiasms in either John 7 or 8, in good scientific fashion I formulated several *hypotheses* that guided further analysis. First I proposed that the

---

1. For example, Bultmann imagined that John 10:1–18 has been extensively cut-and-pasted, but Kim states that "vv. 1–16 are exceptionally adroit in design," and I suggest that vv. 1–18 are united as a single chiasm. Bultmann, *Gospel*, 360; quoted in Kim, *Sourcebook*, 310–11. Kim's scheme does differ from mine.

2. Of course, such an emphasis on the chiastic form in no way limits the variety of approaches by which we may seek to understand Scripture, or the richness of themes that are not identified as contributing to the chiastic structure.

PREFACE

chiastic structure would be present—cruciform structures seemed to be prevalent in surrounding chapters, and I expected them here as well.³ Second, given that chiastic structures did not seem to be present in chapters 7 or 8 separately, there would be a chiastic unit that crossed the chapter boundary.⁴ Third, the story of the woman charged with adultery (7:53—8:11), which occurs at various places in ancient manuscripts, does not belong in its current location, and in fact obscures the original structure. The structure of Jesus' conversation would be revealed if the story of the adulterous woman was bracketed out for convenience.

It was gratifying to find these hypotheses supported by the discovery of a chiasm that extended from 7:14 to 8:59. The whole unit described Jesus' preaching (and his debating with powerful detractors) in the temple during the Festival of Shelters. It became clear to me that the conversation was all one of a piece.

I can make no claim to New Testament scholarship. The summary schemes that I have produced have been paraphrased using a number of translations. English-language translations (especially those like the GNT that aim for maximum clarity by departing from Greek syntax) may not reflect the underlying structures in the original language. The chiastic schemes I have depicted have been abbreviated to various extents for convenience. It remains absolutely essential to read the Gospel of John while considering the suggested arrangements that follow.

Indeed if this study does no more than to provoke more intensive reflection on this Gospel, it will have achieved a valuable function. We are presented with themes—truth, love, unity, joy, a divine quality of life—that people desperately need, even as they engage frantically in distracting or displacement activities.

Sincere thanks are due to the congregations of Trinity at Waiake and the Global Congregation in the Auckland Baptist

---

3. The conversation following the feeding of the crowd of five thousand people (ch. 6) and in the healing of the man born blind (ch. 9) form pronounced chiastic structures.

4. Interestingly, Kim finds a chiastic structure in John 7:10–52. See Kim, *Sourcebook*, 210.

Preface

Tabernacle Church, and to their servant leadership, for giving me the encouragement to study and the opportunity to speak on the wonders to be found in the Gospel of John. May John's testimony to Jesus continue to foster the faith that is needed to receive God's gift of eternal life.

I also sincerely thank Professor Paul Trebilco for providing me with resources and for cautious encouragement to write for fellow laypeople. I hope that he is not disappointed that I have not sufficiently heeded his concerns.

ABBREVIATIONS

GNT   Good News Translation
JB   Jerusalem Bible
JBP   J. B. Phillips New Testament
NIV   New International Version
RSV   Revised Standard Version

1

INTRODUCTION

The Gospel of John[1]

SCHOLARS OF DIFFERENT SHADES have long argued about the class of literature (genre) best used to categorise John's Gospel, but of recent times it has been classified firmly as first-century *bios*, the account of the life and influence of a person of significance. Today we would call it a biography.[2] It is about Jesus. Not surprisingly, the leading question that runs through the whole Gospel is about his identity: Who is Jesus?[3]

Significantly, the Gospel claims to be written by an eye-witnesses of the career of Jesus.[4] In addition, the writings of John frequently refer to a first-person plural "we." Bauckham argues that this "we" is a reference to the author, and the plural is used to emphasize the authority of his eyewitness reporting. It is very much like the "royal we" by which a monarch refers to himself or

---

1. Unless indicated otherwise, Scripture quotes are the author's paraphrase based on the GNT, JB, RSV, JBP, and NIV. References to the original Greek are taken from *The RSV Interlinear Greek-English New Testament*, translated by Alfred Marshall.
2. Burridge, *What Are the Gospels?*, 213–32.
3. For example, Ford, *Gospel of John*, 4, 44, 49, 51–52.
4. John 1:14, 19:35, 21:24; cf. Bauckham, *Eyewitnesses*, 358–63, 368.

A Way of Reading John's Gospel

herself.[5] The emphasis on authoritative testimony means the Gospel does not consist of legends that have evolved over generations of contributors or editors, people whose compositions reflect their pious imaginations. It is not the product of a committee. It is the solemn record of a witness. That sense of immediacy makes the Gospel very special. It takes us, the readers, into the very presence of Jesus and of those who knew him.

Who was this John, whose name is associated with the book? John was a common name, and the one who claims to be the author does not divulge his identity in the text of his Gospel. He seems to refer to himself as "the disciple whom Jesus loved."[6] At other times an anonymous disciple appears in the narrative who may have been the same person.[7]

Traditionally, the author has generally been assumed to be John the son of Zebedee, a fisherman of Galilee and one of Jesus' twelve apostles. Many scholars of the top rank still believe this to be true.[8] Of recent times, other scholars have questioned this assumption and have suggested alternative authors.[9]

The early church leader Papias of Hierapolis (who died about the year 130) described how the teachings of Jesus had been transmitted to him by several people, including two who were named John. There was John the apostle (the son of Zebedee) and John the Elder. Papias wrote as if John the apostle had spoken in the past (i.e., had died) but that John the Elder was still speaking. It seems as if Papias's life overlapped with that of John the Elder in the late part of the first century.[10] It is this John who could have been the

---

5. Bauckham, *Eyewitnesses*, 370–83; see John 1:14, 3:11 (where the speaker giving solemn testimony is Jesus), 12:38 (a quote from Isaiah where the testimony is that of Jesus), 21:24; 1 John 1:1–5, 4:14; and 3 John 12.

6. John 13:23–25; 19:26–27; 20:2–8; 21:7, 20–24. This is the way by which this self-reference is given typically by the GNT and NIV.

7. John 1:35–37, 18:15–16, 21:2.

8. Wenham and Walton, *Exploring*, 276–78.

9. Marsh, *Saint John*, 21–25; du Rand, *Johannine Perspectives*, 75–91; Wright and Bird, *New Testament*, 652–60.

10. Bauckham, *Eyewitnesses*, 15–18; Wright and Bird, *New Testament*, 656–60.

INTRODUCTION

author of John's Gospel. Interestingly, two brief letters in the New Testament, which have a style similar to that of John's Gospel, have been ascribed to someone called John the Elder.[11]

The writer knew Jerusalem and its environs very well and he may have been a resident of Jerusalem.[12] Most of his account is centered in Jerusalem rather than in Galilee. In John's Gospel, we read of several locations in Jerusalem that are not mentioned in any other Gospel. These include the Sheep Gate, Bethzatha, the pool of Siloam,[13] Solomon's Portico, the *wadi* Kidron, the garden beyond it, Gabbatha, and the Stone Pavement.[14] The writer knew Jerusalem as it was before AD 70, the year in which the Romans destroyed the city. Only John mentions the town Ephraim (described as being located near the desert),[15] about twenty kilometers north of Jerusalem.

The writer of John's Gospel gives less prominence (than do those of the Synoptic Gospels)[16] to the twelve apostles. However, he does feature disciples of Jesus who were resident in, or near to, Jerusalem. These disciples include Nicodemus and the siblings Martha, Mary, and Lazarus.[17] He was also personally acquainted with the high priest in Jerusalem, and appeared to have ready access to the courtyard of the high priest's house.[18] He knew the name of at least one of the high priest's slaves (Malchus)[19] and of that person's family connections.[20]

---

11. 2 John 1, 3 John 1.

12. Bauckham, *Testimony*, 15, 177.

13. The remains of the pool were unearthed only in 2004; see "Siloam Pool," para. 2.

14. Bauckham, *Testimony*, 98.

15. John 11:54.

16. The Synoptic Gospels include Matthew, Mark, and Luke, which are structured similarly to each other and contain much of their texts in common—hence, *syn-* (together) and *-optic* (seeing).

17. Bauckham, *Eyewitnesses*, 414; Bauckham, *Testimony*, 177.

18. John 18:15–16.

19. John 18:10.

20. John 18:26.

A Way of Reading John's Gospel

It is plausible that the author John, "the disciple whom Jesus loved," and who reclined next to Jesus at the Last Supper, was the owner of the house (or a member of the household) in Jerusalem in which the last supper was celebrated.[21] From the cross, Jesus committed his mother to the care of this particular disciple, and *from that time* (hour) she lived with him in his home, the immediacy suggesting a Jerusalem location.[22] We have been very close to the action. Perhaps this disciple was much later called "the Elder."

It may be significant that the two sons of Zebedee were distinguished from two anonymous disciples at the lakeside when the resurrected Jesus appeared to his disciples.[23] "The disciple whom Jesus loved" was also present and, as the author of John's Gospel has never named himself, it seems natural to associate "the disciple whom Jesus loved" with one of the two anonymous disciples to the exclusion of John the son of Zebedee.[24]

John's Gospel presents the divine nature of Jesus in very explicit terms. Many scholars have assumed that John's Gospel presents such an exalted view of Jesus only because it reflects the end result of a protracted period in the development of Christian thought. This idea was taken to suggest that John's Gospel was written too late to be the work of an eyewitness.[25] But more recent research has shown that the converse is true: according to ancient conventions, it was only the eyewitness who could interpret the history he was reporting. Mere historians were obliged to limit themselves to the facts that were handed down to them. Bauckham summarizes the eyewitness role thus: "The high degree of interpretation is appropriate precisely because [John's] is the only one of the canonical Gospels that claims eyewitness authorship."[26]

---

21. Bauckham, *Testimony*, 177.

22. John 19:26–27; cf. Acts 1:12–14. This passage implies the mother of Jesus was resident in Jerusalem.

23. John 21:2.

24. Bauckham, *Testimony*, 76–77.

25. Marsh, *Saint John*, 29–30.

26. Bauckham, *Eyewitnesses*, 411.

2

PATTERNS IN THE TEXT

ACCORDING TO THE EXPERTS, John's Gospel is written in straightforward Greek. "This Gospel is a text that has proved to be both accessible to those reading it for the first time and increasingly challenging the more it is reread."[1] But sometimes the flow of the narrative is hard to follow. It seems difficult to discern where it is going, and it often appears to be repetitive. As New Testament scholar Kim Sang-Hoon states, its vocabulary is simple, but readers, even scholars, are often confused by "the complexity of styles, repetition, duplication, and seemingly distracting structures."[2]

Of course, the writer was a Jew who lived in the first century and I am a culturally limited European who writes in the twenty-first century. I have not learned Hebrew or Greek. It follows that I will be unfamiliar with writing styles and conventions that would have been used by contemporaries of Jesus. Kim states that "our first task is to admit that John's way of writing differs from any of today's styles and structures."[3] A necessary task will be to identify the special stylistic features used by Jewish writers such as John.

Jews often wrote using direct parallelisms. They are readily apparent in the Psalms and other Hebrew poetry. A clause or sentence is repeated, and the second iteration tends to emphasise

---

1. Ford, *Gospel of John*, 3, 40.
2. Kim, *Sourcebook*, 1.
3. Kim, *Sourcebook*, 8.

or intensify the idea introduced in the first. The Old Testament scholar Tremper Longman discusses the example of Ps 6:1–2.

> O LORD, do not rebuke me in your anger
>   or discipline me in your wrath.
> Be merciful to me LORD, for I am faint;
>   O LORD heal me, for my bones are in agony.[4]

There are two doublets in this extract. The first contains the related terms "rebuke" and "discipline" on the one hand, followed by "anger" and "wrath" on the other. The second pleads for "mercy" and "healing," for the poet confesses to be "faint" and in "agony." The second line of each doublet tends to take the idea forward. For example, "discipline" is a stronger term than mere (verbal) "rebuke," and "agony" more intense than the feeling of being "faint."[5] As might be expected of a writing that is demonstrably Jewish, John's Gospel contains numerous parallelisms.

Another feature of Jewish writing was the use of *chiasms* (or sometimes, *chiasmus*). These are also called cruciform structures. This is a form of parallelism which possesses a mirror image pattern. A series of ideas may be presented (ABCD) which is then repeated in reverse order (D'C'B'A') so that, for example, A and A' have some similarity in subject matter to each other. These textual forms may also be called inverted parallelisms.[6]

Brouwer has defined chiasm as "the literary flow of a passage in which each element of the first half of the poem or story or discourse is mirrored in a similar element in the second half, inverted in order. Most often, though not always, a center element will be unparalleled, and will carry a unique statement of the most significant idea intended by the author."[7]

Chiasms are layered, somewhat like an onion. To understand what they are getting at, it may be useful to investigate the layers one by one. We necessarily start at the outermost layer (A and A' in the pattern above) and work our way into the center. Another

---

4. Longman, *Psalms*, 95.
5. Longman, *Psalms*, 98.
6. Bailey, *Paul*, 36.
7. Brouwer, "Understanding Chiasm," 100.

analogy may be to say that the elements of a chiasm are nested, one inside the other, like a set of Russian dolls.

Chiasms are mentioned in introductory textbooks on the styles of the biblical writers.[8] They have been explored in studies by the New Testament scholar Kenneth Bailey. He identified numerous chiasms and analyzed their use in the Gospels[9] and in the writings of Paul. As an example, Bailey argues that a chiastic structure gives order to the first letter to the Corinthian church,[10] and it is found in numerous subsections of that letter.[11]

Paul's second letter to Corinth also contains remarkable chiastic structure (2 Cor 1:12—7:16).[12] Read in a (Western) linear fashion, this passage has been considered to be a disjointed jumble, but it is elegantly, cohesively integrated when read as chiasm. Brouwer's scheme is presented in figure 1. Surely this highly structured text is the product of one highly organized mind, and not a hodgepodge of uncoordinated corrections and "improvements" by a tradition of amateurish editors.

A 1:12-22 Corinthians can boast in Paul
　B 1:23—2:11 grief, comfort over painful letter, hope for forgiveness
　　C 2:12-13 looking for Titus in Macedonia
　　　D 2:14—4:6 contrasts: belief/unbelief, believers as God's letters, in glory transformed into God's image
　　　　E 4:7—5:10 triumph over hardship
　　　　　F 5:11-21 ministry of reconciliation
　　　　E 6:1-10 triumph over hardship
　　　D 6:11—7:4 contrasts: belief/unbelief, believers as God's temple, in light transformed into his holiness
　　C 7:5-7 finding Titus in Macedonia
　B 7:8-13a grief, comfort over painful letter, joy after forgiving
A 7:13b-16 Paul can boast in Corinthians

Figure 1. Paul's Sorrow, Triumph, and Work[13]

8. Longman, *Psalms*, 101–2.

9. Bailey, *Jesus*.

10. Bailey, *Paul*, 26.

11. For example, Bailey, *Paul*, 73 (1 Cor 1:21–26a); 107 (1 Cor 2:7–10a); 183 (1 Cor 6:13–20).

12. Brouwer, "Understanding Chiasm," 116.

13. Modified from Brouwer, "Understanding Chiasm," 116.

A Way of Reading John's Gospel

A challenging section of Paul's letter to the churches at Rome (chs. 9–11) addresses the issue of God's continuing care for the Jewish people. It is also arranged as a chiasm.[14] Wright has highlighted this arrangement but does not provide neat headings for each element. I have attempted to resolve the inherent pattern that he describes (fig. 2). It commences and concludes with worship (doxology), and then works through the difficult question of God's purposes for the Jews and the gentiles. It centers on the proclamation that all who believe God raised Jesus from death, and who confess Jesus is Lord, will be saved—that is, they will be instated as members of God's chosen people.

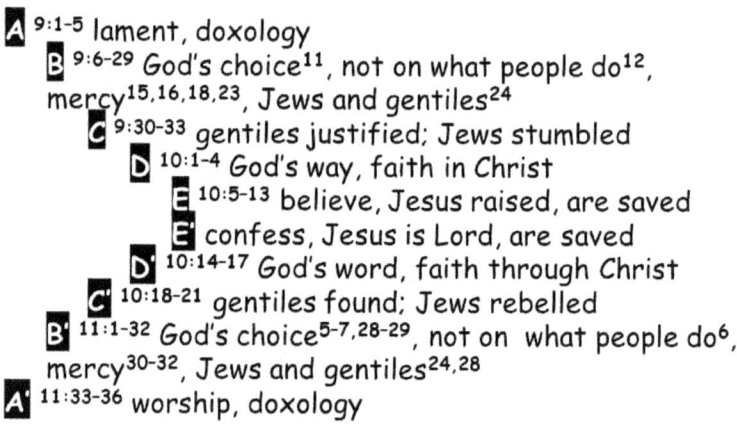

A 9:1-5 lament, doxology
  B 9:6-29 God's choice[11], not on what people do[12], mercy[15,16,18,23], Jews and gentiles[24]
    C 9:30-33 gentiles justified; Jews stumbled
      D 10:1-4 God's way, faith in Christ
        E 10:5-13 believe, Jesus raised, are saved
        E' confess, Jesus is Lord, are saved
      D' 10:14-17 God's word, faith through Christ
    C' 10:18-21 gentiles found; Jews rebelled
  B' 11:1-32 God's choice[5-7,28-29], not on what people do[6], mercy[30-32], Jews and gentiles[24,28]
A' 11:33-36 worship, doxology

Figure 2. Jews and Gentiles Are Saved on the Same Basis[15]

Returning to John's Gospel, we note that it is known to possess significant chiastic arrangements. A striking example is John's description of seven (what we might label as) miracles. However, John calls them "signs" (Greek, *semeia*).[16] They probably identify

14. Wright, *Paul*, 1163; Wright and Bird, *New Testament*, 520–22.

15. Superscripted numbers following key words or phrases indicate the verse(s) that contain(s) them. Developed from Wright, *Paul*, 1163, and Wright and Bird, *New Testament*, 520–22.

16. Wright and Bird, *New Testament*, 665–67.

a diversity of matters that are significant to the message of the Gospel. Jesus' works of healing "are signs of the presence of the kingdom of God," displaying "the healing compassion of God that characterises the kingdom."[17] They highlight various aspects of the great transformation that God is effecting by means of Jesus: "new creation, new dimensions to God's work, new Exodus, new life, new light."[18] In other words, they are the first inklings that God is acting to make a new world in which the pain, suffering, and sin of our old world will be excluded.

Jesus' signs also carry messages about who he is. They "show Jesus to be the Savior" because they provide "concrete demonstrations of his power to give life."[19] Even more than that, John presents the signs as pointers to Jesus' divinity.[20] In the service of another theme in John's Gospel, the "seven signs manifest Jesus' glory so that people may believe in him."[21] John is concerned, not just with the events themselves, but with what they point to, the glory of God.[22]

And why are there seven such signs? In Jewish thinking, "seven" points to perfection and completion (as with the seven days of the creation story). The mission of Jesus involves re-creation, and his signs show that *new creation* is going to take place.[23] The signs are organized in a chiastic arrangement, as is given below. The verses indicated in parentheses identify them as signs.

   1 water to wine (2:11)
     2 healing of boy close to death (4:54)
       3 cripple at pool of Bethzatha (6:2)
         4 feeding five thousand men (6:14, 26)
       5 blind man at pool of Siloam (9:16)
     6 raising of Lazarus from death (12:18)

17. Bauckham, *Jesus*, 55.
18. Wright, *John, Part 2*, 37.
19. Bauckham, *Testimony*, 244.
20. Wenham and Walton, *Exploring*, 257, 261.
21. Bauckham, *Testimony*, 274; Harris, *Raised*, 29.
22. Rae, "To Render Praise," 201–20.
23. Rae, "To Render Praise," 201–20.

A Way of Reading John's Gospel

7 crucifixion and resurrection (2:18–19)

Rae points out that, in true chiastic style, sign 1 corresponds to sign 7, 2 with 6, and 3 with 5. Sign 4 is without a parallel, and is located at the center, the apex, of the overall structure. Rae has identified several features common to the parallel stories.[24]

Signs 1 and 7 (table 1) both feature a *third day*, which is a symbol that something momentous is about to happen: "on the third day, there was a wedding" and on the third day Jesus rose from the grave. Jesus uses the term "woman" to refer to Mary only in these stories—a tender form of address that anticipates the abandonment of Jesus. The expression "my hour has not yet come" (2:4) foreshadows the time when his hour had come, the crucifixion (17:1). The stories feature transformations, of water to wine and of the water of purification ceremonies (pertaining to the old earth) to the joy and freshness of new creation (sign 1). And the transformation of water to the wine of the new world (2:8–9) occurs only by the shedding of blood and water from Jesus on the cross, the washing that removes sin (13:8–18, sign 7).

Table 1. Transformation of the Old Creation to the New (Signs 1, 7)

Sign 1. Water into wine (John 2)	Sign 7. Jesus' death, resurrection (John 18–21)
a wedding on the third day (2:1)	resurrection on the third day (19:42—20:1)
out of wine (2:3)	cheap wine (19:28–30)
Jesus addresses mother as "woman" (2:4)	Jesus addresses mother as "woman" (19:26)
the hour not yet come (2:4)	the hour had come (12:27, 13:1, 17:1)
water to wine (2:8–9)	blood and water (19:34)
Jesus revealed his glory (2:11)	Jesus revealed his glory (13:31)
disciples believed (2:11)	disciples believed (16:14, 14:23–23)

The key thought to be found in signs two and six is not healing from bodily disease, but the giving of life! Jesus' authoritative

---

24. Rae, "To Render Praise," 201–20.

pronouncement in the first story is "Your son will live!" (4:51)[25]; in the second it is "Your brother will rise to life!" (11:23). The signs celebrated Jesus' victory over death and culminate in Jesus' claim to be the "resurrection and the life."[26]

Table 2. Jesus' Authority over Life and Death (Signs 2, 6)

Sign 2. Healing of the Boy (John 4)	Sign 6. Raising of Lazarus (John 11)
Jesus spent two days in Samaria (4:43)	Jesus spent two days by Jordan (10:40, 11:6)
the boy was sick (4:46)	Lazarus was sick (11:3)
return to Galilee, but not respected (4:44)	return to Judea, but might be stoned (11:7–8, 16)
Jesus: "Your son will live" (4:50–51, 53)	Jesus: "Your brother will rise to life" (11:23)
people believed (4:48, 50, 53)	people believed (11:15, 45)

The two healing stories (signs three and five) have so much in common that we cannot doubt that they are intended to be read in parallel. They occur at two of Jerusalem's famous pools. In each, Jesus comes across a man with a long-term physical affliction: one is lame, the other blind. Jesus heals them, but on the Sabbath day, and elicits the ire of religious rigorists. In the resulting controversies, Jesus warns of judgment.

Table 3. Jesus Highlights Spiritual Blindness (Signs 3, 5)

Sign 3. Healing of the lame man (John 5)	Sign 5. Healing of the blind man (John 9)
pool of Bethzatha (5:2)	pool of Siloam (9:7)
Jesus saw the man (5:6)	Jesus saw the man (9:1)
condition for thirty-eight years (5:5)	condition since birth (9:1–2)
healing on Sabbath (5:9–10, 16)	healing on Sabbath (9:14)
Jewish authorities angry (5:10, 15, 18)	Jewish authorities angry (9:16–18, 22)
man did not know who Jesus was (5:13)	man did not know who Jesus was (9:36)

25. Marsh, *Saint John*, 68.
26. Rae, "To Render Praise," 201–20.

Jesus converses afterwards (5:14)	Jesus converses afterwards (9:35)
in temple (5:14)	in synagogue (9:22, 34)
believing in Jesus (5:24)	believing in Jesus (9:35, 36, 38)
Jesus as judge (5:22, 27, 30)	Jesus as judge (9:39, 41)

In sign four, God overcomes inadequacy of human provision and replenishes the fruits of land and sea.[27] But more than that, Jesus shows that he is the bread that gives life (6:26–27). The food provided in the desert in Moses' time was of great importance to Jews (a historical instance of God's care), but it was just a pointer to the spiritual bread that gives the fullness of life. John's Gospel does not describe the Lord's Supper (as the Synoptic Gospels do). However, the explanation of the Lord's Supper is given here (6:53–58). *Eating Jesus' flesh* means accepting that his sacrificial death was on our behalf.

As will be shown later, the text describing Jesus' teaching arising from sign four itself is organized as a chiastic structure, and the center of this center is a powerful statement of Jesus' mission. The Father's will is that Jesus should give eternal life to those who believe in him, and that he will resurrect them on the day when God acts definitively to complete his work in the world (6:39–40). This sign points forwards to the cross because people wanted to make Jesus king (6:15), although they totally misunderstood the meaning of Jesus' kingship (18:36). Jesus is declared in many ways to be king when he is crucified.

We might also discern different patterns of the way chiasms are presented. These will be suggested in the text below.

First, there are (what we might call) stand-alone chiasms, often with a seven-fold symmetry (after Bailey).[28] For example, the famous story of the woman charged with adultery (John 7:53—8:11) is a single unit that manifests a symmetrical structure.

---

27. Rae, "To Render Praise," 201–20.

28. Bailey, *Jesus*, 138, 196, 239, 324, 355. Bailey refers to this seven-fold symmetry as the "prophetic rhetorical template." He spells the structure out further as "the seven-scene 'ring composition' style traceable to the writing prophets" (Bailey, *Jesus*, 239).

Second, there are occasions when chiastic arrangements seem to be paired. The first depicts an event or conversation, and the second draws out the theological implications of the first. Such a pattern seems to be a feature of Jesus' conversations with Nicodemus, with the Samaritan woman, and with Jesus' disciples on the day of his resurrection.[29]

Third, in some cases, the chiastic structure occupies an entire chapter, or it extends across chapter boundaries. A famous instance that is well known by scholars, is found in the trial of Jesus before Pilate.[30] This carefully constructed block of text might have made a far more natural (and helpful) chapter unit than that disrupted by the arbitrary chapter division as given in our Bibles. It appears that the Lord's high priestly prayer[31] may also, in its entirety, be organized into a chiasm.

Fourth, there is evidence that large-scale arrangements of the Gospel also follow a chiastic structure. Kim believes that the overall structure of John's Gospel is chiastic.[32] He argues that the central part (X) is not the "center of significance" but the link that connects the other parts of the text.[33]

> A introduction (1:1–51)
>   B1 Cana cycle (2:1—4:54)
>   B2 festival cycle (5:1—10:42)
>   X link (11:1—12:50)
>   B'1 Farewell Discourse (13:1—17:26)
>   B'2 passion narrative (18:1—19:42)
> A' conclusion (20:1—21:25)

As mentioned above, the arrangement of the seven signs described in the Gospel is chiastic. And I will propose that the

---

29. The conversations are found, respectively, in John 3, 4, and 20 (both the paired stories involving Mary and the paired stories involving the apostles on resurrection day).

30. John 18:28—19:16; see also du Rand, *Johannine Perspectives*, 21, and Kim, *Sourcebook*, 14.

31. John 17.

32. Kim, *Sourcebook*, 22–31.

33. Kim, *Sourcebook*, 22–23.

wonderful conversation of Jesus with his disciples on the night of his betrayal—known as the Farewell Discourse—can be divided into sections that fit together with a seven-fold chiastic structure.

The overall impression from all this is that the ancient Jews were amazingly sophisticated writers. They were literary craftspeople, almost incredibly attentive to textual arrangement, at least from our perspective. Almost unconsciously, perhaps, they produced texts of complex and elegant form. Why did they use chiasms? Does the form of a text—in our case, its mirror image structure—matter in practical terms?

First, parallel statements support each other. We might miss the import of a statement when we read it a first time, but when we come upon it a few lines later, it can arrest our wandering thoughts. The idea is repeated, and this reiteration ensures that there is mutual reinforcement.

Second, the center of a chiasm often expresses the thought that is the climax of the paragraph. Here we can find an important idea that the writer seeks to impress upon his readers. In fact, one way by which I have discovered candidate chiasms is to note paired (directly parallel), important statements that encapsulate major aspects of John's theology. I have then worked outwards from this center and discovered parallels in the surrounding text.

Third, chiastic structures may be a footprint of a prior period of verbal preaching. We can expect John to have preached the story of Jesus over many years, and the strongly patterned structure by which his content was arranged represented a mnemonic device—a help to the memory—as he discoursed without written notes. It is only natural to propose that when John finally committed his lifelong sermons and teaching to written form, he maintained the same structure. After all, it was deeply embedded in his mind.[34] If John did in fact write his Gospel in the nineties of the first century, we can be sure that his memory would have been

---

34. This was suggested to me by my pastor, theologian Dr. Craig Heilmann. But Brouwer says as much when he writes that chiasm is "an expression of oral rhetoric and literary design in ancient poetry and short-story telling." Brouwer, "Understanding Chiasm," 99.

well served by the frequent repetition of his artfully constructed material. Alternatively, the use of chiasm may have been adopted to enable readers (or listeners) to memorise the text more easily and to gain greater insight into what is written.

For us, lay readers who seek to understand John's Gospel in the twenty-first century, the recognition of chiastic units may assist in our efforts. The text is so rich, beautiful, inspiring, even overpowering in its impact, and we might feel lost. Part of my work on this book was done in Cambridge, England, and, while there, I wandered through beech forest. Every noble tree, the cascading undergrowth, the path winding through the verdure enthralls the senses—but it is so easy to get lost by taking wrong turnings. I have found the analysis of chiasms helpful in mapping out the landscape in John's Gospel. It helps to identify units of text, the development of ideas, explain repetitions, and highlight pronouncements of seminal importance.

Identifying chiastic units thus assists the reader in recognizing the natural boundaries of modules in the text composing John's Gospel. By observing such units, readers may identify the introductory information, key themes, and the trajectories of their development, climactic statements, and applications that are peculiar to each such unit. Hopefully it may help teachers to be more effective.

3

JOHN 1

Divine Word and Human Witness

THE FIRST CHAPTER OF John's Gospel has been arranged to incorporate three separate sections. It describes Jesus' *divinity*, John the Baptist's *declaration* about Jesus, and the earliest calls to *discipleship*.

JESUS' DIVINITY

The first eighteen verses constitute the prologue of the Gospel. They have a pronounced chiastic structure. I was gratified to find that the scholar Sang-Hoon Kim also described the prologue as a chiasm and that it centered at vv. 12–13.[1] My version of the prologue (fig. 3) has the same logic, as described below.

---

1. Kim, *Sourcebook*, 38; see also Brouwer, "Understanding Chiasm," 102.

John 1

A ¹⁻³ In the beginning the Word already existed; the <u>Word was with God</u>; <u>the Word was God</u>. From the beginning the Word was with God. Through him God made all things; not one thing was made without him
  B ⁴⁻⁵ The Word was the source of life, this life brought <u>light</u> to humanity. The light shines in the darkness; the darkness has not overcome it
    C ⁶⁻⁹ God sent his messenger <u>John</u>, as a <u>witness</u> to the light, so that all should believe; he was not the light, came to <u>witness</u> to the light, the true light that comes into the world, enlightens all people
      D ¹⁰⁻¹¹ The <u>Word was in the world</u>; God made the world through him, the world did not know him; he came to his own country, own people did not receive him
        E ¹² Some did receive him, believed in him; he gave them the right to <u>become God's children</u>
        E' ¹³ They <u>were</u> not <u>born</u> by natural means, by a human father; God himself was their Father
      D' ¹⁴ The <u>Word became a human being</u>, full of grace and truth, <u>lived among us</u>; we saw his glory as the Father's only Son
    C' ¹⁵ <u>John</u> gave his <u>witness</u> to him: "This is the one of whom I said: 'He comes after me, is greater than I am, existed before I was born'"
  B' ¹⁶⁻¹⁷ Out of the fullness of his grace he has <u>blessed</u> us all, giving us one blessing after another. God gave the Law through Moses, but <u>grace and truth</u> came through Jesus Christ
A' ¹⁸ No one has seen God. The only Son, <u>who is the same as God</u>, <u>at the Father's side</u> has made him known

Figure 3. Prologue: From God's Son (the Divine Word) to God's Children[2]

The first (vv. 1–3, A) and final (v. 18, A') elements provide combined witness to John's conviction that the Word (Jesus) shares in the divine identity. The opening phrase "In the beginning" is a clear echo of the creation account of Genesis, and God's Word-who-is-Jesus is given an inalienable role in the divine work of creation. The author wants his readers to know that his Gospel is the "story of God and the world. . . . It is about the way in which the long story which began in Genesis reached the climax the creator had always intended."[3] The designation of Jesus as the Word (Greek, *Logos*) carried important connotations for both Greek and Jewish readers.

The author of John's Gospel faced the challenge of proclaiming a Jewish Messiah in a Greek culture. Accordingly, he used the idea of the Word, which Heraclitus (fl. 500 BC) had equated with the Reason of God. It was "the principle of order" by which the ever-changing universe existed, according to which the flow of

---

2. In this and subsequent figures, underlined words or phrases suggest concepts that are present in both elements of a parallel pair.

3. Wright, *John, Part 1*, 3.

events occurred, and by which humans were able to reason.[4] In later Hellenistic philosophy (including that of Plato, the Stoics and Philo), the Word remained the "satisfying rational principle for understanding the universe."[5]

But the essential meaning of the term as used by John is "the divine Word that all Jews, on the basis of Genesis, understood to have been active in the creation of all things. . . . As God's own word, it was intrinsic to God's own unique identity." In the context of the prologue, Jesus the Messiah is identified as God's Word, which was spoken "*within the Genesis creation narrative*" that described the bringing forth of creation.[6] The *logos* can refer to God's expression in the Law or Torah (as with the Ten Commandments or *deka logoi*), the Prophets (who spoke "the word of the Lord") and the Writings (in which it is identified with Wisdom), including the Psalms.[7] It is by God's Word that God accomplishes his will.[8]

The second pair of elements (B, B′) describes how this divine Word has communicated God's message and blessings to humanity. The terrible gap between an unimaginable God and benighted people has been crossed. The Word himself has brought inextinguishable divine light to people (vv. 4–5, B). The understanding of *light* may be enhanced by the acronym LIGHT: Light Is Glory, Holiness, Truth. In the fullness of his grace, he has brought to impoverished humanity blessings, grace, and truth (vv. 16–17, B′).

The third elements introduce the forerunner of Jesus, the rugged prophet John the Baptist, the first person to announce Jesus as the bringer of this light (vv. 6–9, C). In some mysterious way, Jesus is superior to him (v. 15, C′). As human beings, John is older than Jesus, but the text implies that Jesus lived with the Father prior to his appearance as a human person. The claim that Jesus existed before John points to Jesus' incarnation.

---

4. Barclay, *Gospel of John*, 1:11–13.
5. Marsh, *Saint John*, 96–97.
6. Bauckham, *Testimony*, 241 (italics original).
7. Ford, *Gospel of John*, 29.
8. Isa 55:11, Ps 33:6. See Wenham and Walton, *Exploring*, 260.

The fourth elements (vv. 10–11, D; v. 14, D′) draw the concepts stated hitherto into an amazing synthesis. This divine Word, the eternal Creator, became an inhabitant of the world—indeed, a member of the human species, *Homo sapiens*, in a stunning act of incarnation. To Greek readers, the notion that the divine Word should become flesh (*sarx*) was an impossible, "shatteringly new thing."[9] And yet, despite his incomprehensibly gracious initiative of bridging God and humanity, he was ignored by the majority of his countrypeople. But to the author of the Gospel and his colleagues, Jesus showed God's glory. That is, he embodied the very presence of God, at the heart of which is love.[10] As such he was the "Father's only Son" (1:14 GNT).

The central pair of elements (v. 12, E; v. 13, E′) constitute a parallelism and are unified by the idea of *becoming God's children* or *being born* as the children of the divine Father. This is the status and destiny of those who *received* Jesus the Word and who (the theme of John's Gospel introduced in v. 7 and here in v. 12) *believed* in him.

JOHN'S DECLARATION

The testimony of John the Baptist follows in the next section. It also is presented in chiastic form. It seems that the last verse of the prologue also serves as the opening statement of this section (fig. 4).

---

9. Barclay, *Gospel of John*, 1:44–45.
10. Barclay, *Gospel of John*, 1:51.

A Way of Reading John's Gospel

A ¹⁸ <u>No one has ever seen God;</u> only <u>Son</u>, the same as God, at the Father's side, has made him known.
    B ¹⁹⁻²³ delegation to John: "Who are you?"
    John's testimony: "Not the Messiah, Elijah, the Prophet"
    delegation: "Tell us who you are; what do you say about yourself?"
    John: "The voice shouting in the desert; make a straight path for the Lord to travel"
        C ²⁴⁻²⁶ "Why do you baptize?"
    John: "<u>I baptize with water</u>, but among you stands the one <u>you do not know</u>
            D ²⁷ <u>He is coming after me</u>; I am not good enough to untie his sandals"
                E ²⁸⁻²⁹ᵃ in Bethany, east of the Jordan River, where John was baptizing, saw Jesus coming to him
                    F ²⁹ᵇ "Look! the Lamb of God,
                    F' who takes away the sin of the world!
                E' ³⁰ This is the one I was talking about
            D' A man is coming after me; he is greater than I am, he existed before I did
        C' ³¹ <u>I did not know</u> who he would be, but <u>I came baptizing with water</u> <u>to reveal him</u> to Israel"
    B' ³²⁻³³ John's testimony: "I saw the Spirit come from heaven as a dove, rest on him.
I did not know him, but God said to me, 'You will see the Spirit come down, stay on a man; he baptizes with the Holy Spirit'
A' ³⁴ <u>I have seen it</u> - I tell you that he is the <u>Son</u> of God"

Figure 4. The Declaration of John the Baptist

Verses 18 and 34 (A, A′) both play on the concept of *seeing*. No one can *see* God in the incomprehensible transcendence of the divine nature. But, in wondrous contrast, the divine Son has made him known. John has *seen* the divine affirmation of Jesus as the one who gives the Holy Spirit. The two verses together emphasize that Jesus is the Son of God, but not merely in the sense of being a human messiah. He is the Son who is the same as God, at the Father's side, and who—from that unique position of divine authority—has made God known and unleashed the Spirit of God.

The phrases "Father's only Son" (v. 14), "only Son" (v. 18), and "Son of God" (v. 34) are striking. Father-Son terminology is used frequently in this Gospel. How should we understand this group of terms? In the Old Testament (or Hebrew Scriptures), "son of God" was a name given to Israel itself and also to Israel's representative, the king.[11] The term "Son of God" came to be applied to Jesus as designating his messianic kingship. This may be the sense when

---

11. "Son of God" applied to Israel (Exod 4:22–23, Hos 11:1) and Israel's king (Ps 2:7).

people address Jesus, especially in the Synoptic Gospels.[12] In John's Gospel also, when people speak to Jesus, "Son of God" and "King of Israel" or "Messiah" seem to be equivalent terms.[13]

Jesus uses the language of Father and Son extensively. It is clear that he is that Son. Jesus uses the terminology to emphasize his intimacy with God who is Father.[14]

But when the Gospel author reflects on the significance of Jesus, he seeks to emphasize the Son's *eternal* relationship with the Father. This is shown especially when Jesus' role in creation is specified, as in chapter 1 (above). The Son's agency in creation is closely connected with his eternity.[15] Wenham and Walton have written that John uses the term Son of God "in a very strong sense." Jesus is preexistent, "God made audible and made visible."[16] Bauckham summarizes: "In John's Gospel, Jesus is no mere human son of the divine Father, but the eternal Son who has taken on human identity in order to give eternal life to the world. Yet it is through his self-denying obedience to God that Jesus fulfils his identity as the divine Son."[17]

The second and penultimate elements (B and B′) contain John's solemn *testimony* and deal with the question of identity—first of John the Baptist and then of Jesus. John in humility gives himself no title but eventually concedes that he is merely a voice in the desert, acting in preparation of the Lord (vv. 19–23, B). John here quotes from Isaiah, for whom "the Lord" refers to God; but if "this is about testifying to Jesus, then Jesus is being identified with the Lord—that is, with God."[18] However, John is able to announce to the world the identity of the one who provides the promised gift of the Holy Spirit—God's great eschatological gift (vv. 32–33, B′).

---

12. See Matt 16:16, Mark 14:61.

13. For example, as spoken by Nathaniel and Martha: John 1:49, 11:27; see Thurmer, *Son*, 25.

14. Thurmer, *Son*, 29–30, 33–35, 45, 54.

15. See also 1 Cor 8:6; Col 1:15–16; Heb 1:2; Thurmer, *Son*, 47–49.

16. Wenham and Walton, *Exploring*, 260–61.

17. Bauckham, *Jesus*, 91.

18. Ford, *Gospel of John*, 45.

The subsequent elements indicate that John *baptized with water* to address those who did not know the one who stood amongst them (vv. 24–26, C) in order that he would become known (v. 31, C'). Ironically, this special One was *coming after* John, but was superior to John (v. 27, D; cf. v. 30b, D'). Then for the first time in John's preaching, at a specified place and point in history, the man Jesus is named (vv. 28–29a, E) and identified as that exalted person who John sought to introduce (v. 30a, E').

Unsurprisingly, the central climax of the chiasm is John's pronouncement on the mission and nature of Jesus. He is the Lamb of God. He takes away the sin of the world (v. 29). This direct parallelism describes Jesus as a lamb, but not one like those used in the soon-to-be obsolescent sacrificial rituals. As God's eternal Word who is the self-giving Lamb, he acts sacrificially and definitively to deal with the cumulative sin of humankind.

THE CALL TO BE DISCIPLES OF JESUS

The third section in chapter 1 describes the call and witness of the first disciples of Jesus and it also has features of a chiasm (fig. 5). The account commences and concludes with testimonies to Jesus' identity. The one who is the divine Word of God is here identified as the sacrificial "Lamb of God" (vv. 35–36, A) and the royal "Son of God" (v. 49, A'), understood by Nathaniel as the King of Israel.

A ³⁵⁻³⁶ John with two disciples, saw Jesus: "Lamb of God"
  B ³⁷ disciples went with Jesus;
  ³⁸ª Jesus saw them following him: "What do you want?"
    C ³⁸ᵇ⁻³⁹ disciples: "Where do you live?" Jesus: "Come and see"
      D ⁴⁰⁻⁴¹ Andrew found Simon: "We have found the Messiah"
        E ⁴² he took Simon to Jesus; Jesus looked at him: "You will be called Cephas" (which means Peter or rock)
        E ⁴³⁻⁴⁴ Jesus found Philip, said to him, "Come with me!"
      D' ⁴⁵ Philip found Nathanael: "We have found the one of whom Moses and the prophets wrote: Jesus"
    C' ⁴⁶ Nathanael: "Good from Nazareth?" Philip: "Come and see"
  B' ⁴⁷⁻⁴⁸ Jesus saw Nathanael coming to him: "A true Israelite"
Nathanael: "How do you know me?"
Jesus: "I saw you under the fig tree"
A' ⁴⁹ Nathanael: "Son of God, King of Israel"

Conclusion: ⁵⁰⁻⁵¹ Jesus: "Do you *believe* because I told you I saw you under the fig tree? You will see greater things; will see heaven open, God's angels ascending and descending on the Son of Man"

Figure 5. The Calling of the First Disciples

Subsequent elements seem to draw the reader to the act of associating themselves with, and being disciples of, Jesus. Jesus saw people following (or *coming to*) him (vv. 37–38a, B; vv. 47–48, B′). Why did Jesus' statement to Nathaniel ("I saw you under the fig tree," vv. 48, 50 JB) evoke the effusively positive response described in v. 49? It has been suggested that the image of a man under a fig tree carried connotations of peace, of messianic fulfilment.[19] Nathaniel understood the allusion: this man Jesus was heralding the new age for which true Israelites yearned! And Nathaniel responded in kind: Jesus was the longed-for Messiah. In response to questions about Jesus, the reply is the invitation to *come and see* (v. 38b, C; v. 46, C′). Then the neophyte disciples *found* their acquaintances and gave them the extraordinary news that they had *found* the Messiah (vv. 40–41, D; 45, D′).

---

19. 1 Kgs 4:25; Mic 4:4; Barclay, *Gospel of John*, 1:76; Marsh, *Saint John*, 148.

A Way of Reading John's Gospel

The central elements do not seem at first glance to be particularly striking. But they seem to present Jesus himself as the one who takes the initiative of gathering disciples. First, Jesus renames Simon (v. 42, E). He is to be known as Cephas (Aramaic, *Kepha*), the Rock. Is the lesson here that people find their true identity when they become disciples of Jesus? We twenty-first century people may seek our identity in nationality, race, sexuality, occupation, or culture. But these are but accidents of our birth or of our environment. Our self-worth and true potential are found in an appropriate response to the call of Jesus. And here, Jesus gives Cephas (or *Petros*, in the Greek translation) his new identity. He is going to be a pillar in Jesus' new community. When, after the resurrection, Jesus appeared to Mary of Magdala, he conferred her true identity also upon her (see 20:16, discussed in ch. 16).

Second, Jesus combines the sense of *finding* Philip and calling him to *come with me* (vv. 43–44, E'). In the surrounding verses, the men talking about Jesus had engaged in extensive *finding* and *coming*. Here those same terms are used of Jesus. Ultimately, he is the supreme finder of human beings, the unique leader or shepherd who calls them to come after him. The sheep are saved only in his finding of them and their coming to him.

Following the end of the chiastic structure is a summary statement that draws attention to John's thematic message to his readers: the imperative to *believe*. As is often the case, there seems to be steps in believing, a progression toward full, unswerving commitment to Jesus, as he is progressively revealed to us.[20] John wants the reader to take note: there is much more to be learned about this man Jesus. Finally, Jesus alludes to the story of Jacob's ladder in the Hebrew Scriptures.[21] Jesus is now that ladder, the locus of communication between God and humanity. And, in a more genuine sense than in that ancient story, Jesus himself is now

20. It is helpful to recognize that John's Gospel "describes many ways and stages of believing, and its approach to believing and trusting makes room for questioning, doubting, ambiguity, testing, gradual as well as sudden realization, growing, and maturing." Ford, *Gospel of John*, 40, 75, 302–3, 324–25.

21. See Gen 28:12–19, where Jacob dreamed of a ladder to heaven and named the place "Bethel."

Bethel (house of God), the place where God lives, the temple, as will be portrayed in the next chapter.[22]

---

22. Ford, *Gospel of John*, 58–59.

4

JOHN 2

Transformation of the Old Age to the New Age

THE SECOND CHAPTER OF John describes two events. Each narrative is arranged in a chiastic pattern. The first one relates Jesus' actions to prevent a potentially embarrassing catering mishap at a rustic wedding celebration. This is the story in which Jesus changed water into wine.[1] This action is said to be the first of Jesus' seven signs (Greek, *semeia*). According to Stephen Verney, it is the first (Greek, *arche*) in both temporal sequence and in power.[2] It is the sign that is paradigmatic of the transformation of the old order of creation to the new creation.

Somewhat strangely, in the second story, the scene changes from a peasant wedding to the supreme festival of Jewish faith, the Passover. We translocate from a small town in Galilee to the center of Israel's religious, cultural, and political life—the temple in Jerusalem. Jesus' action in the temple provides the occasion in which Jesus identifies, and looks forward to, the seventh sign: the destruction and transformation of his own body, the New Temple.

---

1. This story is described as a chiasm also by Kim, albeit with a slightly different structure to that presented below. See Kim, *Sourcebook*, 76–77, 86.
2. Verney, *Water into Wine*, 35.

JOHN 2

WATER INTO WINE

The story about the wedding features the idea of *becoming* (Greek, *ginomai*). It follows as a sequel to the prologue of the previous chapter. All things *came into being* through him (1:3). The world *came into being* through him (1:10). He gave power to *become* children of God (1:12). The Word *became* flesh (1:14), and grace and truth *came* through Jesus Christ (1:17). Similarly, the creative Word transformed water into (it *became*) wine (2:9). We may characterize events as ordinary or extraordinary, but they all equally reflect the God who acts in freedom, creativity, and generosity.[3]

The narrative describing Jesus' sign at the wedding feast can be arranged as a chiastic structure (fig. 6). The first (vv. 1–2, A) and last (vv. 11–12, A′) elements of the chiasm are about the facts of the event. In the town of Cana in Galilee, a wedding was attended by Jesus, his mother, and the disciples. But the last element has two vital developments. First, Jesus revealed his glory. Verney indicates that "glory" meant "the weight of a thing, and so its value" and also its "brightness." In this story, glory indicates Jesus' true worth shining out in such a way that people could see it.[4] Second, the disciples, in some sense, believed in him.

---

3. Ford, *Gospel of John*, 64–65.

4. Verney, *Water into Wine*, 36; similarly, Ford defines glory as "the overflowing radiance, intensity, and energy of divine life and holiness," and this is redefined and intensified as "the love of Jesus embodying the love of God." See Ford, *Gospel of John*, 265–66.

A Way of Reading John's Gospel

A ¹⁻² wedding in <u>Cana in Galilee</u>; <u>Jesus' mother</u>, Jesus and <u>disciples</u> invited
  B ³ <u>wine</u> given out, Jesus' mother: "They are out of <u>wine</u>"
    C ⁴⁻⁵ Jesus: "Is that our concern? My hour has not come."
    Jesus' mother <u>told</u> servants, "Do whatever he <u>tells</u> you"
      D ⁶ six stone water jars, used by Jews for ceremonial
      washing, were there, each holding twenty to thirty gallons
    C' ⁷⁻⁸ Jesus <u>told</u> servants: "Fill jars with water;" they filled them;
    he <u>told</u> them "Draw some out, take it to the man in charge;"
    they took him the water
  B' ⁹⁻¹⁰ which had become <u>wine</u>; he did not know where it had come
  from; called the bridegroom: "Everyone else serves the best <u>wine</u>
  first, then inferior <u>wine</u>; you have kept the best <u>wine</u> until now"
A' ¹¹⁻¹² Jesus performed this first miracle in <u>Cana in Galilee</u>; revealed his glory, disciples *believed* in him; <u>Jesus and his mother</u>, brothers, <u>and disciples</u> went to Capernaum

Figure 6. The Wedding Feast: From the Water of Ritual to the Wine of Celebration (Sign 1)

The second (v. 3, B) and penultimate (vv. 9–10, B') elements report the story about the crisis and its resolution. They are about *wine*, consumed, exhausted, and then replenished. The latter element is elaborated with a subtle irony: it is the wine that Jesus provides that is the best. This is perhaps a gentle nod to the idea of the messianic banquet: the longed-for celebration at the consummation of history, when God would at last act to restore his people.

The third (vv. 4–5, C) and fifth (vv. 7–8, C') elements describe Jesus' authority. The key feature is what Jesus *tells* the servants to do. They obey when they carry out what they are *told* to do. For the reader, the message is clear: the people of Israel will be blessed only when they obey this unexpected Messiah. We readers too are blessed only when we accept the divine summons to follow and serve this Lord.

The central, unpaired element (v. 6, D) appears to be a mere explanation of the way Jews engaged in ritual washing. What is this bit of background cultural information doing in the center of the story? Perhaps it is crucial—as we might suspect of an element at the center of a cruciform. "The water jars are a sign . . . that God is doing a new thing from within the old Jewish system, bringing purification to Israel and the world in a whole new way."[5] The theological point that the author is making is that the unfulfilling repeated activity of ritual washing (the *water*) has been superseded by the joyful realization of the kingdom of God being inaugurated by the Messiah (the celebratory *wine*). Jesus is providing a wedding celebration with a vengeance—not merely for a young man and a young woman but for the true bridegroom and bride, the Messiah and the renewed people of God.[6]

THE TEMPLE: TORN DOWN AND REBUILT

Much of John's Gospel story is set in the context of Jewish annual celebrations. The Passover Festival is mentioned here, in John 6, and it was the occasion of Jesus' final visit to Jerusalem.[7] In addition to Passover, John's Gospel also relates events during the Festival of Shelters,[8] the festival of the dedication of the temple,[9] and another celebration that is unspecified.[10] In John's Gospel, Jesus fulfils the symbolism of the rituals traditionally enacted at the festive occasions.[11] As Wright says, this emphasis "locates the ministry of Jesus in terms of Jewish sacred time." Jesus is bringing "Israel's history towards its intended goal." John evokes cherished scenes from Israel's history "in order to say: all this is now reaching its appointed fulfilment."[12]

In the Synoptic Gospels, Jesus' final (Passover) visit included an act of judgment on the temple. This is probably the same event as that described in John 2.[13] Perhaps John juxtaposes the wedding and

---

5. Wright, *John, Part 1*, 22.
6. Marsh, *Saint John*, 142–43, 146.
7. John 12:12, 13:1, 18:28.
8. Also known as Succoth, this festival is featured at length in John 7–8.
9. Also known as Hanukkah; see John 10:22.
10. John 5:1.
11. Wenham and Walton, *Exploring*, 260.
12. Wright, *New Testament*, 412.
13. Marsh, *Saint John*, 157–58; Wright, *Jesus*, 425.

temple stories because they both illustrate the passing of one order and the inauguration of a new one. The transformation is from ceremonial washing to the celebration of the messianic age; from the backward-looking Passover to a new and greater Passover heralding the new exodus to be achieved by Jesus. The related themes are renewal (or renovation) and replacement, from old to new.[14]

A possible structure of this pericope is depicted in figure 7. The narrative starts (2:13–16, A) and ends (2:23–25, A′) by specifying that Jesus was in Jerusalem during the Passover Festival. As is John's standard practice, the final element concludes with a summary of those who, in some sense, had come to believe in him.

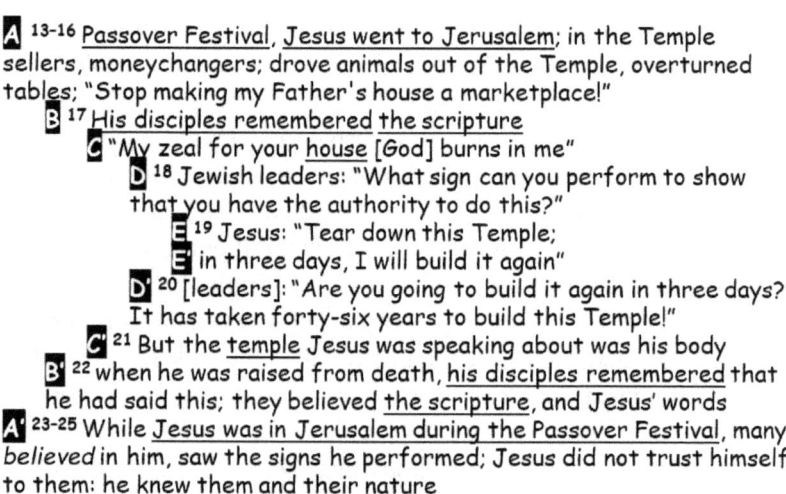

A 13-16 Passover Festival, Jesus went to Jerusalem; in the Temple sellers, moneychangers; drove animals out of the Temple, overturned tables; "Stop making my Father's house a marketplace!"
  B 17 His disciples remembered the scripture
    C "My zeal for your house [God] burns in me"
      D 18 Jewish leaders: "What sign can you perform to show that you have the authority to do this?"
        E 19 Jesus: "Tear down this Temple;
        E in three days, I will build it again"
      D′ 20 [leaders]: "Are you going to build it again in three days? It has taken forty-six years to build this Temple!"
    C′ 21 But the temple Jesus was speaking about was his body
  B′ 22 when he was raised from death, his disciples remembered that he had said this; they believed the scripture, and Jesus' words
A′ 23-25 While Jesus was in Jerusalem during the Passover Festival, many believed in him, saw the signs he performed; Jesus did not trust himself to them: he knew them and their nature

Figure 7. Passover: Transitioning from the Old to the New Exodus
(Defining the Future, Sign 7)[15]

---

14. Kim, *Sourcebook*, 24, 74–76.

15. The GNT expresses the Jewish authorities' question (v. 18) as, "What miracle?" However, their actual word is sign: "What sign [*semeion*]?" Jesus answered by speaking of his future death and resurrection (tearing down and rebuilding his body, the true temple). This identifies Jesus' death and resurrection as sign 7.

The subsequent elements feature recollections of the disciples as these recollections related to Jesus and the temple. When Jesus enacted judgment on the temple, they *remembered* the Scripture that spoke of fierce devotion to God's house (v. 17, B). They failed to understand what they were observing but later *remembered* Jesus' veiled depiction of his resurrection: the temple to be torn down and raised was Jesus' own body (vv. 21–22, B').

And the authorities asked for a miracle, a sign (v. 18, D), while wholly failing to understand what that sign would be (v. 20, D'). The central statement is Jesus' deeply ironic prediction of the tearing down and rebuilding of the temple (v. 19, E, E'). It is ironic because it was universally misunderstood as referring to the magnificent building that Herod had constructed. At his trial before the Jewish council, these words were cited as evidence of Jesus' seditious intent toward Israel's cherished institution.[16] However the figurative referent was Jesus' own body: he himself is the true temple in whom God lives, the *place* where God can be encountered. And the *tearing down* and *rebuilding* referred to the sacrifice of Jesus' body in death and the transformation of that body in resurrection.

To summarize, the first story describes Jesus' first sign (v. 11). The second describes (in figurative terms) and anticipates the sign that will be Jesus' last and greatest (vv. 18–28): the destruction and reconstruction of the true temple, the body of Jesus, in sacrifice and resurrection (as described later in chs. 19–20).

---

16. Mark 14:57–59. Jesus' words were somewhat corrupted by the witnesses; see also Matt 26:61; Wright, *Jesus*, 166, 335.

5

JOHN 3

Spiritual Birth to Eternal Life

THIS CHAPTER CONTAINS SOME of the most well-known verses in the Bible. It has three chiastic structures, the first of which describes a conversation with an uncomprehending questioner and the second of which draws the theological applications from the first. The third is a commentary on what John the Baptist had to say about Jesus. The two sections establish Jesus as the one "who has come down from heaven" (v. 13), that is, "the one who God has sent" (v. 17).

JESUS AND NICODEMUS

Jesus' conversation partner is called Nicodemus. This is a Greek name and means "conqueror of the people,"[1] hardly a modest way of introducing oneself. But John makes it clear that the name fits the person. Nicodemus was wealthy[2] and influential, probably as a member of the Jewish council (the Sanhedrin).[3] This story also

---

1. Bauckham, *Testimony*, 161.

2. John 19:39. Nicodemus brought to Jesus' tomb a weight of spices that implies extreme wealth (Bauckham, *Testimony*, 163).

3. Marsh, *Saint John*, 173; cf. John 7:45–52.

identified him as a member of a rigorous religious group, the Pharisees (v. 1), and as a respected scholar (v. 10).

The Hebrew equivalent of the name was the very rare Naqdimon. Bauckham has pointed out that the ancient Jewish records identify a family, which bore the name Gurion, in which there were two people known as Naqdimon. This family was fabulously wealthy and located socially in the Jerusalem aristocracy.[4] Names tended to be reused in families, and Bauckham proposes that the Nicodemus who came to see Jesus was a member of this ruling family, a third bearer of the name Naqdimon.

But Nicodemus came to see Jesus at night.[5] A possible structure of the dialogue is depicted in figure 8. The conversation started with what he *knew*: he confessed Jesus as *a teacher sent by God* (v. 2, A). It seems to finish with a gentle and ironic prod from Jesus (vv. 9–10, A′), in the light of what Nicodemus *did not know*: that a spiritual birth was essential for membership in God's kingdom. Nicodemus was also (renowned as) *a teacher of Israel* but was in truth ignorant about the fundamental need of a spiritual birth.

---

4. Bauckham, *Testimony*, 137–72. Bauckham observes that "male names were repeated across generations in upper-class Jewish families of this period" (149).

5. Reasons for the nocturnal visit are not known. Was it to avoid censure or persecution? Or to ensure an uninterrupted conversation? Bauckham, *Testimony*, 165. Perhaps there is symbolism as well: "Nicodemus would have come to Jesus from that world of darkness in which the true light of God was now pleased to shine." Marsh, *Saint John*, 174.

A Way of Reading John's Gospel

¹⁻² Nicodemus, leader, Pharisee: to Jesus one night

A Nicodemus: "<u>We know</u> <u>you are a teacher</u> sent by God
No one could perform signs unless God were with him"
  B ³ Jesus: "No one sees God's Kingdom unless <u>born</u> again"
    C ⁴ Nicodemus [surprise]: "A grown man, <u>born again</u>?"
      D ⁵ Jesus: "No one enters God's Kingdom unless
      <u>born of water and the Spirit</u>
        D' ⁶ <u>born physically of human parents</u>; <u>born</u>
        <u>spiritually of the Spirit</u>
    C' ⁷ Do not be surprised: all must be <u>born again</u>
  B' ⁸ like the wind, everyone <u>born</u> of the Spirit"
A' ⁹⁻¹⁰ Nicodemus: "How?"
Jesus: "<u>You are a teacher of Israel</u>—<u>you don't know</u> this?"

Figure 8. Entry into God's Kingdom Requires
Both Physical and Spiritual Birth

The conversation introduced Jesus' teaching on the need to be born again (or born from above). Birth dependent upon God as Father has been introduced in the prologue (1:12–13). This second birth is a requirement of seeing God's kingdom (v. 3, B). And it is actualized by God's Spirit (v. 8, B').

Nicodemus's response evinces his incredulity at Jesus' notion of a second birth, which he understood in terms of biological birth, parturition (v. 4, C). Jesus patiently tells him not to be surprised as Jesus emphasizes that being "born again" is an essential event (v. 7, C') involving, as the crux of the conversation makes clear, a nonphysical transformation.

The center of the chiasm is a direct parallel. Jesus explains that two births are required for people to attain the full humanity that God intends for them. There is birth of water and of the Spirit (v. 5, D). There is birth of a physical nature and of a spiritual nature (v. 6, D'). This clarifies what "birth by water" means. It refers to the amniotic fluid bathing a fetus and the dramatic "breaking of the waters," which is an early event in the birth process.⁶ So people enter into a human family by biological birth. But all people may be made new spiritually—coming to possess the very life of the triune God, and so entering the divine family—through the work of God's Spirit. This birth effects a change in their values and loyalties, their relationality and their whole personality and being.

The second chiasm follows directly from the first (fig. 9). It expounds the implications of the concepts described in the conversation with Nicodemus. The first (v. 11, A) and final (vv. 19–21, A′) elements both deal with the claim that Jesus speaks of what he knows (he has brought light), but has been met with the people's general unwillingness to respond appropriately to that truth. People are *not willing* to accept (v. 11) or to come to (v. 20) that light. Jesus stated emphatically that he had come as Savior, not as judge (see below). But people's *response* to the light he has brought—typically, they scurry into the darkness—reveals their misplaced loyalties. They judge themselves.[7] "Not to trust oneself to God's love is a self-judgment and of course means that there cannot be a life of love together."[8]

---

6. Another biological fluid described as "water" was that which flowed when the side of Jesus was pierced by a spear (John 19:34). In this case, "blood and water" referred to the red settled erythrocyte component and the protein-rich, straw-colored plasma, respectively, that proved Jesus' blood had decomposed and that he was dead. Another meaning of the "water" may be an echo of Ezek 36:24–28, which points to the promised cleansing of the heart by the Holy Spirit. See Wenham and Walton, *Exploring*, 266.

7. Verney, *Water into Wine*, 51, 88.

8. Ford, *Gospel of John*, 99.

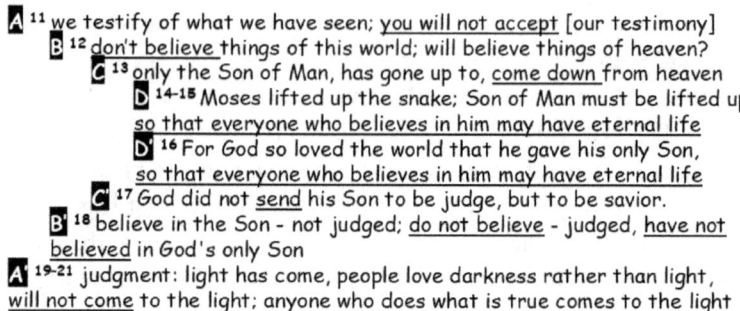

Figure 9. Receiving Eternal Life Requires that People Believe in the Son

The second (v. 12, B) and penultimate elements (v. 18, B') explicate the nature of the people's rejection of his message: it is a refusal to *believe*. Jesus then spells out how he, the Son of Man (v. 13, C) and Son of God (v. 17, C') is indeed the very emissary of the Creator God. Jesus has come down from heaven; he has been sent by God. That Jesus has been *sent* is fundamental to the way he understands his relationship with the Father and to his own self-identity.[9]

The center of the chiasm consists of two closely parallel statements that explain how the unique Son is God's life-giving gift. Everyone who believes has eternal life (vv. 14–16, D, D'), which is effectively the same as entering into God's kingdom (vv. 3 and 5 of the previous chiasm). This is the first time in John's Gospel that the themes of God's love and eternal life have been explicitly mentioned. Eternal life is received *at the time* of believing in Jesus. It is not merely life after death.[10] Bauckham has explained how in

---

9. Verney, *Water into Wine*, 64, 174. That Jesus has been *sent* is first mentioned in John's Gospel in 3:17; it is repeated in 3:34; 4:34; 5:24, 30, 36, 37, 38; 6:38, 39, 44, 57; 7:16, 28, 33; 8:16, 18, 26, 29; 9:4; 10:36; 11:42; 12:44, 45, 49; 13:20; 14:24; 15:21; 16:5; 17:3, 8, 18, 21, 23, 25; 20:21. Analogously, "the disciple whom Jesus loved" perhaps may reveal the author's self-consciousness, the primary feature of his lived experience. How is our self-consciousness, our fundamental identity, expressed? The person who has received God's grace?

10. Ford, *Gospel of John*, 96.

the Gospels, the possession of eternal life and entering into God's kingdom are interchangeable, synonymous terms.[11] These key statements (believing, receiving eternal life) embody the theme of John's Gospel.[12]

In this central direct parallelism, we also have the first of three occasions in which John's Gospel expresses the idea of the Son of Man being *lifted up*.[13] In the prosaic sense, it refers to something being raised or elevated, as when a man was subjected to crucifixion. In the figurative sense, as Harris observes, it indicates the conferment "of highest honor and supreme power." In John's Gospel "the literal and figurative uses are blended to great effect. The crucifixion is seen as simultaneously man's act of lifting Jesus up on a cross to die and God's act of lifting Jesus up to a place of supreme glory and lordship."[14]

The other key term in the central parallelism cites those who "believe" (Greek, *pisteuein*). How should this *believing* be understood? It requires that people *see* or *perceive* that Jesus, when lifted up, reveals the very essence or apogee of God's love and mercy. In addition, it means people trust themselves to the Truth revealed, entering into a dialogue with the transforming Love manifested. And further, it means to start acting in accordance with what is seen.[15] As Ford expresses it, in John's Gospel, *pisteuein* means "believing truths, trusting in a person, and committing one's life to someone."[16]

JESUS AND JOHN THE BAPTIST

The final section of John 3 (vv. 22–36) considers the relationship between Jesus and John the Baptist. The latter person is farewelled

---

11. Bauckham, *Testimony*, 111–12.
12. John 20:31.
13. Besides John 3:14, see 8:28 and 12:32–34.
14. Harris, *Raised*, 77.
15. Verney, *Water into Wine*, 49.
16. Ford, *Gospel of John*, 95, 149.

at this point. Jesus and John were baptizing people at the same time. The narrative specifies John's location (Aenon near Salim, where there was water) and the phase of his work (before he was imprisoned). John's followers seemed to be concerned at the apparent competition arising from the coincident operation of the two reforming prophets. John's response and the author's reflection describe the absolute supremacy of Jesus the Messiah, as presented in a possible chiasm, hidden in the concluding part of the chapter (fig. 10).

A 27 John: "No one can have <u>anything</u> unless <u>God gives</u> it
  B 28 You are my witnesses, I said: 'I am not the Messiah; I <u>have been sent</u> ahead of him'
    C 29 The bride belongs to the bridegroom; the bridegroom's friend listens, rejoices when he hears the bridegroom's <u>voice</u>—my joy is made complete
      D 30 He must become greater; I must become less"
      31 <u>He who comes from above is greater than all.</u>
      D' He who is from the earth belongs to the earth, speaks about earthly matters, <u>but he who comes from heaven is above all</u>
    C' 32-33 He tells what he has seen and heard, yet no one accepts his <u>message</u>; whoever accepts his <u>message</u> confirms by this that God is truthful
  B' 34a The one whom <u>God has sent</u> speaks God's words
A' 34b-35 because <u>God gives</u> him the fullness of his Spirit. The Father loves his Son; has put <u>everything</u> in his power.

36 Summary: Whoever *believes* in the Son has eternal life; whoever disobeys the Son will not have life but remain under God's punishment

Figure 10. John the Baptist Is Farewelled; Jesus' Supremacy Is Affirmed

At the outset, John stated that people (referring to himself?) cannot have *anything* apart from what *God gives* (v. 27, A). The paragraph concludes that Jesus the Messiah has power over "everything," and possesses the fullness of God's Spirit, as a result of what *God gives* (vv. 34b–35, A'). John's prophetic commission, and Jesus' messianic one, are both given, ordained by, God.

Moving into the onion, this contrast between John and Jesus is reinforced. John *has been sent* ahead of Jesus the Messiah (v. 28, B). He is a servant, but Jesus *has been sent* to deliver God's very words (v. 34a, B').

The next pair of elements consider the effects of Jesus' words, his message. John is merely the bridegroom's friend, and he feels privileged to listen to the bridegroom's voice—and in so doing, he rejoices (v. 29, C). Jesus' words, his testimony, demonstrated the truth of God to that small number of people who take them to heart (vv. 32–33, C′).

The center of the chiasm (vv. 30–31, D, D′) contains a direct parallelism, which clinches the difference between John and Jesus. John's role is to fade away; Jesus' role is to grow in people's appreciation and estimation. These divergent fates fill John with joy. Given the parallel nature of these verses, John may have been humbly describing himself as earthly ("he who is from the earth," v. 31 GNT), and his service of preaching repentance as earthly. The origins of Jesus however are heavenly, from the presence of God, and he is uniquely qualified to speak of transcendent realities. These would include revelations about the Father, the Spirit, eternal life, and the new people of God who will be called to live in love and unity.

This block of text concludes, as is typical of this Gospel, with a summary statement of the importance of believing in Jesus (v. 36). This solemn statement is a direct recapitulation of key verses, vv. 15 and 16.

6

JOHN 4

Life-Giving Spirit, Life-Giving Son

THIS CHAPTER IS ORGANIZED around two interactions. First, Jesus had a conversation with a Samaritan woman, someone at the bottom of the social ladder (at least from a Jewish perspective). Second, there was an engagement between Jesus and someone of rather greater prestige: an official, possibly in the Roman or Herodian administration. Either way, these different people showed the same exemplary response to Jesus' challenge to them.

JESUS AND THE SAMARITAN WOMAN

By the standards of the day, Jesus' dialogue with a Samaritan woman was scandalous, not merely because Jews and Samaritans did not talk to each other but—particularly (!)—because the Samaritan was a *woman*. She was probably also a social outcast, as she came to the well in the heat of the day presumably to avoid other people. As in the previous chapter, a prior conversation (with an uncomprehending person) is presented as a chiasm (fig. 11) and is followed by its explication, also expressed as a chiasm.

JOHN 4

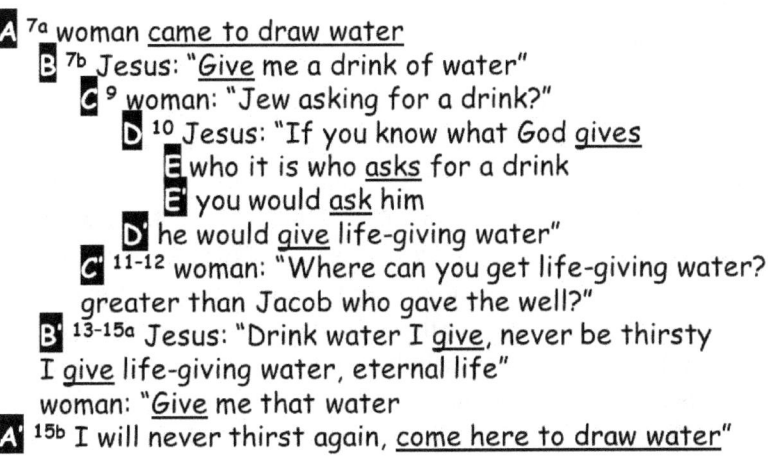

Figure 11. Jesus Gives Life-Giving Water

The text starts at Jacob's well. This landmark is unambiguously identifiable today and is near Mount Gerizim, the site of worship that is sacred to Samaritans. A woman came to the well to draw water (v. 7a, A). It ends with her misplaced hope that she would never again have to come to the well to draw water (v. 15b, A'). As with Nicodemus, she has failed to understand Jesus' metaphor.

The second and penultimate element are about *giving water* to drink. Jesus' conversation-starter was to request a drink from the well (v. 7b, B). In the corresponding element below (vv. 13–15a, B'), Jesus offered to give water but of a kind that quenches thirst permanently. This water is life-giving and sustains eternal life. The woman missed the point, and she asked Jesus to give that mysterious water to her.

The next elements express the woman's perplexity (v. 9, C; vv. 11–12, C'). Who is this man? What sort of water is he talking about? Does he think that he is greater than Jacob?

The central section is about God's gift: *life-giving water*, a term that is introduced at this point and repeated in the elements below. Although chiasms are symmetrical in form, new ideas (in this case, life-giving water) are often introduced in the second half.

Jesus challenged the woman to consider who he is, and to "ask" for that life-giving water (v. 10).

The text moves on from Jesus' thirst-quenching metaphor, which was wholly obscure to the woman. There is a delightful irony in the outermost layer of the second chiasm (fig. 12). In the first element, Jesus requested the woman to go, call her husband, and *come back* (vv. 16–18, A). At the end of the text, the woman obeyed (vv. 28–29, A'). She went back to the town, and summoned ("*come* and see," v. 29) not just her husband but the entire populace. In my mind's eye I see them streaming from the town toward the well, and the crowd includes not just a husband but a group of men who have been her husband and the *de facto* partner as well. Jesus and his message so impressed her that her evangelizing enthusiasm exceeded his initial command. Jesus rejected the chauvinism of his day to commission a woman to be his true witness to the Samaritans, just as in resurrection, Mary Magdalene was to be the true witness to the apostles.[1]

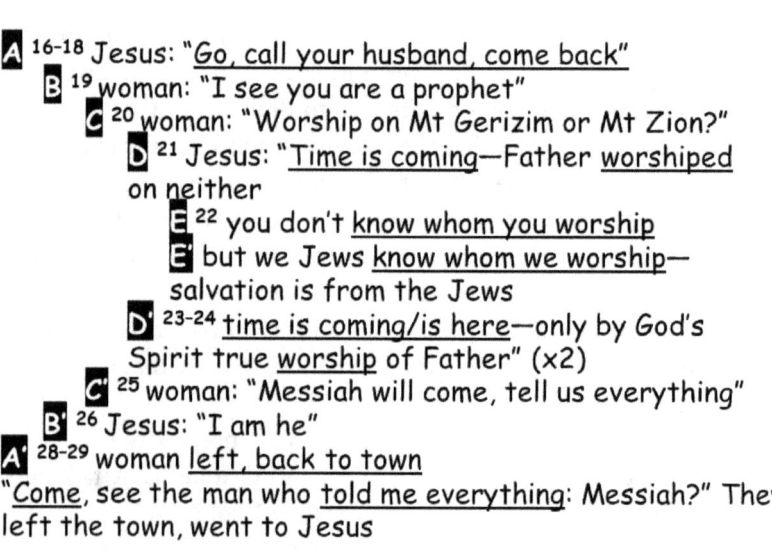

Figure 12. Jesus Inaugurates the True Worship, Enabled by God's Spirit[2]

1. Bailey, *Jesus*, 208.
2. Jesus' first absolute "I am" statement is given (v. 26).

JOHN 4

The second and penultimate elements pertain to the identity of Jesus. The woman ventures that this man is a prophet (v. 19, B). Jesus acknowledges to her that he is the Messiah (v. 26, B'). But a deeper meaning may be discerned when Jesus tells the woman, "I am he" (Greek, *ego eimi*).[3] This is the first of seven incidents (note the special number) in the Gospel where we encounter the term "I am he." These are known collectively as absolute "I am" sayings.[4] It is very much like a Hebrew term used in Isaiah by which God announces his presence and his saving authority to the people.[5] The seven-fold absolute "I am" sayings of John's Gospel thus indicate that Jesus' identity is shared with God. Jesus is more than a prophet, even more than a human messiah; he is to be understood as bearing the authority and status of God. As Bauckham states, "The 'I am he' declarations are among the most emphatically monotheistic assertions of the Hebrew Bible, and if Jesus in the Fourth Gospel repeats them he is unambiguously identifying himself with the one and only God." Jesus has the authority to offer the Samaritan woman the living water that gives eternal life; he is "truly God in the fullest sense."[6]

Perhaps the woman sought to deflect the conversation by airing her theological uncertainties. She first raised the vexed question of the mountain upon which God should be worshiped (v. 20, C). Jews and Samaritans had fought bitter wars over this issue. She later attempted to shelve the hard questions by postponing them to the time when the Messiah would at last come (v. 25, C').

Jesus brought the conversation to a head, as expressed in two parallelisms. The theme of true worship occupies the D/D' and E/E' elements. First, *the time will come* when sacred mountains—Gerizim or Zion—will be irrelevant to the question of true worship (v. 21, D). Shockingly (for any Jew) Jesus asserted that the

---

3. Bauckham, *Testimony*, 244, 248.

4. John 4:26; 6:20; 8:24, 28, 58; 13:19; 18:5-8; Bauckham, *Testimony*, 244-46.

5. Deut 32:39; Isa 41:4; 43:10, 13, 25; 46:4; 48:12; 51:12; 52:6; Bauckham, *Testimony*, 246-48.

6. Bauckham, *Testimony*, 247-48.

special status of Jerusalem and its temple (and therefore its sacrificial system and priesthood) would soon abolished. He could say that to a Samaritan—but would have been lynched on the spot if he had said that in a Jewish setting! Indeed, *the time will come*—it is already here—when God's Spirit alone will enable true worship (vv. 23–24, D'). This is repeated for emphasis. The sole venue for true worship would be the adoring heart of the forgiven sinner, in which the Spirit of God is resident.

Second, Samaritans *did not know whom they worshiped*. Jews *did know whom they worshiped* (v. 22a, E; v. 22b, E'). God's eschatological age had come. That age with its longed-for salvation would arrive not through the formalities of Samaritan religion but through God's faithfulness to the covenant he made with the Jews. The Samaritans revered the books of Moses but not the Psalms and the Prophets, which pointed Israel to God's salvation, effected by Jesus. As Philip said in the earliest days of Jesus' mission: "We have found the one of whom Moses wrote about in the book of the Law and whom the prophets also wrote about."[7]

A key aspect of this conversation seems to require resolution. In the first part (fig. 11) the climax has Jesus emphasizing the need for life-giving (living) water. In the second part (fig. 12), it is the Spirit of God who is central. The living water and the Spirit are not explicitly identified with each other. But we may infer that the living water is a metaphor for the life-giving, worship-enabling Holy Spirit because these themes occupy equivalent parts of their respective chiasms. The link is made explicit only later in the Gospel.[8]

The Samaritan episode finishes, as is the pattern in this Gospel, with a statement that the Samaritans have come to *believe* in Jesus (vv. 39–41). The nature of their faith is to acknowledge Jesus as the *Savior of the world* (v. 42)—not merely of the Jews but of all humanity. The gentile mission is underway. The title "Savior of the world" is used only here in John's Gospel, and "is not a typical

---

7. John 1:45; see also Luke 24:27; Acts 3:24–25.
8. John 7:37–39.

JOHN 4

messianic designation in the first century." However, the title was also used for the emperor of Rome.[9] Usurping Caesars should beware!

THE OFFICIAL'S SON

The final pericope[10] of chapter 4 describes Jesus' healing of a boy. This is a dramatic story that makes perfect sense when read linearly, but perhaps it shows chiastic character (fig. 13). The first (vv. 43–46a, A) and last (v. 54, A′) elements provide the setting (in Galilee), refer back to sign 1 (water to wine) and identify this current healing as the second sign. We are also presented with the seemingly anomalous statements that Jesus was not *respected* but he was *welcomed*. In other words, people were not interested in Jesus himself, the one to whom the signs pointed, but they were eager to see more of his signs merely as spectacles in themselves.[11]

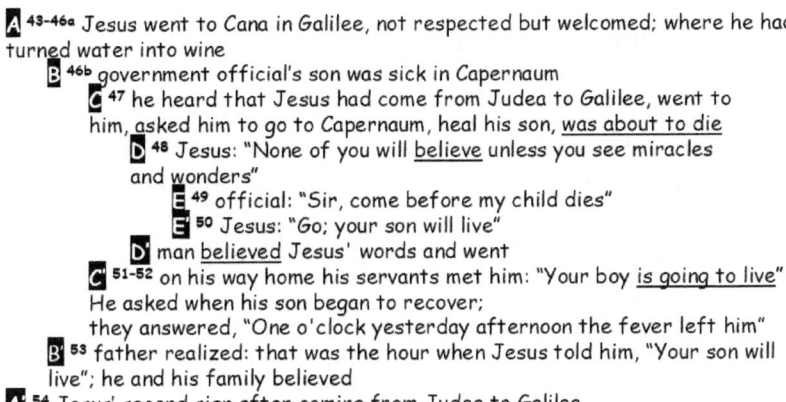

Figure 13. Jesus' Power over Life and Death: The Boy at Capernaum (Sign 2)

---

9. Koester, *Savior*, 665.

10. A *pericope* is a demarcated unit of text in the Gospels, whether of narrative or of teaching.

11. Wright, *John, Part 1*, 52–53.

A Way of Reading John's Gospel

In the first half of the chiasm, three of the elements describe the severe sickness of the boy (vv. 46b, 47, 49; B, C, E). The corresponding elements in the second half of the chiasm all describe how Jesus ensured that the boy would live (vv. 50, 51, 53; E', C', B'). The death-life dichotomy is presented in the central elements (vv. 49–50). As described earlier, this story is about more than Jesus' ability to heal; it is about his authority over life and death, which is why this healing story forms a pair with the raising of Lazarus (sign 6).[12]

Finally, the theme of believing is presented in the paired elements (v. 48, D; v. 50b, D') that are found on each side of the central pair. Jesus indicated how hard it was to show genuine faith, but the official showed exemplary faith by obeying when Jesus sent him home. Unlike most other Galilean people, he believed in the words of Jesus (or, we might say, in the Word who is Jesus) before any dramatic sign was presented to him. And as we have come to expect, the theme of faith is raised at the end of the pericope, closing chapter 4 (v. 53). The official and his family perceived from the sign the true identity of Jesus.

Chapters 3 to 4 have described how Jesus finds believers from widely disparate social groups, including a Jewish aristocrat, a Samaritan outcast, and an official who is probably employed in Roman or Herodian government. The rest of his public work (chapters 5 to 12) describe debates about Jesus' identity and about the life he gives. These arguments seem to become progressively more heated.[13]

---

12. See signs 2 and 6 as discussed in Rae, "To Render Praise," 201–20.
13. Ford, *Gospel of John*, 123–24.

7

JOHN 5

Lord of the Sabbath I: Opposing Spiritual Deadness

WE COME TO THE third of Jesus' signs, the healing of a crippled man at the pool of Bethzatha, back in Jerusalem. The pool is described as having five colonnades and, as shown by its ruins visible in Jerusalem today, four of those colonnades form a rectangle around the whole complex, whilst the fifth separates a north from a south pool.[1] This story and its aftermath develop with the use of three chiasms.

The first narrative unit commences (v. 3, A) and ends (v. 13, A') with a crowd (fig. 14). It presents a man who had been unwell for thirty-eight years (v. 5), and it closes with the warning that disobedience to God results in effects that are more cataclysmic than mere physical sickness (v. 14).

---

1. This detail demonstrates that the author of John's Gospel really knew Jerusalem as it existed before the Romans destroyed the city in AD 70.

A Way of Reading John's Gospel

1-2 Setting: Jerusalem, a festival, Bethzatha

A ³⁻⁵ large crowd; man sick 38y
  B ⁶ Jesus' question: "Do you want to get well?"
    C ⁷ man: "I have no man to help"
      D ⁸ Jesus: "Pick up mat, walk"
        E ⁹ picked up mat, walked (a Sabbath)
      D′ ¹⁰ leaders: "Against our law to carry your mat
    C′ ¹¹ man: "The man who made me well told me"
  B′ ¹² leaders' question: "Who told you?"
A′ ¹³⁻¹⁴ crowd, Jesus slipped away; "Do not sin again, or something worse may happen"

Figure 14. Sabbath Healing at Bethzatha (Sign 3)

The second (v. 6, B) and second-to-last (v. 12, B′) elements are questions addressed to the sick man. The man answers initially that he has no one to help him (v. 7, C); and later, that there was One who made him well (v. 11, C′). When he seemed to be alone in the world, engagement with the one man Jesus made all the difference.

The center of the pericope describes Jesus' command to the lame man (v. 8, D), the religious leaders' criticism of that command (vv. 9b–10, D′), and the healing that followed obedience (v. 9a, E). According to Wright, when Jesus commanded the crippled man to get up (v. 8), he was using a word often used to describe the resurrection. This sign was not a singular, isolated instance of power; it demonstrated that Jesus was introducing "a new life, a new creation"—the new world that God had always intended to bring about.[2]

The account of the miracle and its hostile reception is followed by Jesus' affirmation that the Father and he, the Son, act in absolute unison (v. 17). This claim provoked an angry response from the authorities—the first of the major disputes about the

---

2. Wright, *John, Part 1*, 57.

JOHN 5

unique relationship of the Father and the Son. It was also the first occasion when the authorities were said to want him dead (v. 18).

Jesus' response is presented in the form of another chiasm (fig. 15). The first (vv. 19–20a, A) and last (v. 30, A') elements state clearly that the Son "can do nothing on his own." Father and Son act together. The Son *does* only what the Father *does*. The Greek word translated "does" (*poiein*, in each instance) also carries the meaning of "makes" or "creates,"[3] providing echoes of the prologue ("not one thing in creation was made without him," 1:3).

A 19-20a Truly, "The Son can do nothing on his own; does only what his Father does; the Father loves the Son, shows him all that he does
  B 20b-21 you will be surprised: as the Father raises the dead, gives life, the Son gives life
    C 22-23 nor does the Father judge anyone, has given his Son the right to judge, so all will honor the Son as they honor the Father
      D 24 Truly: those who hear my words, believe in him who sent me have eternal life, will not be judged, have already passed from death to life
      D' 25-26 Truly: the time is coming—has already come—when the dead will hear the voice of the Son of God, will come to life; as the Father is the source of life, he has made his Son to be the source of life.
    C' 27 [the Father] has given the Son the right to judge, because he is the Son of Man.
  B' 28-29 do not be surprised: the time is coming when the dead will hear [the Son's] voice, leave their graves: those who have done good will rise, live; those who have done evil will rise, be condemned
A' 30 I can do nothing on my own; I judge only as God tells me; I seek not my own will, but the will of the one who sent me"

Figure 15. Sabbath Healing: United Work of Father and Son

The second (v. 21, B) and second-to-last (vv. 28–29, B') elements specify a particular activity in which the Father and the Son act in unison. As the Father raises the dead and gives them life, so does the Son. As Wright says, the "*work of raising the dead has already begun.* . . . The present 'resurrection,' the new birth during

---

3. Ford, *Gospel of John*, 130.

the present life, finally produces the future bodily resurrection that will correspond to Jesus' own."[4] The work of raising the dead is the prerogative of God alone. The Son shares the divine prerogative of giving life to the dead.

Further divine prerogatives, possessed by the Father and given to the Son, follow in the next pairs of elements. These include the right to judge, which is associated with the right to receive honor (vv. 22–23, C; v. 27, C').

The center of this pericope has two directly parallel elements that emphasize the divine authority of the Son. The (spiritually) dead will *hear the words* (echoing the *logos* again) or the *voice* of Jesus, the Son of God; and those who hear will receive life (v. 24, D; vv. 25–26, D'). To receive this life is a concomitant of escaping judgment (v. 24). God's promises are being fulfilled *now* in the vocation of Jesus. As Jesus stated to the Samaritan woman, "the time has already come" (v. 25; cf. 4:23). God's gift of eternal life is being made available through Jesus' activities.

It seems as if Jesus' teaching, like his healing sign, has been rejected. His discourse continues in a more polemical tone in a third chiastic arrangement (followed by a concluding mini-chiasm, fig. 16). Jesus starts by allowing (according to Jewish convention) that to speak on his own authority does not have legal force (v. 31, A).[5] And he chides his audience that time and again they will accept some pretender who, on that con man's authority alone, demands and receives their loyalty (v. 43b, A').

---

4. Wright, *John, Part 1*, 63–64 (italics original).

5. Marsh, *Saint John*, 268. Even further, one can only make a valid claim to be divine if God gives his testimony to that claim.

JOHN 5

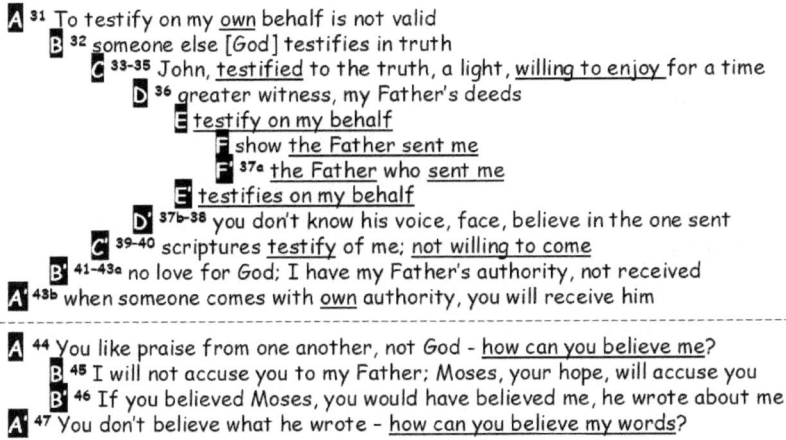

Figure 16. Sabbath Healing: Heed the Witnesses

The second (v. 32, B) and penultimate (vv. 41–43a, B′) elements identify the other, supreme witness to Jesus' authority. Jesus' authority is from God. That is implied in v. 32 and stated explicitly in v. 43. Scholars differ as to whom the "someone else" (v. 32) refers: Is it God or John the Baptist who is cited in the following verses?[6] Jesus' witness in v. 32 seems to be God himself, because (if the pericope is indeed a chiasm) the parallel element (v. 43) refers to the authority conferred upon Jesus by the Father. Moreover, the witness (v. 32) is given in the present tense; the Baptist's witness in the following verses (vv. 33–35) is in the past tense,[7] and we may suppose that he is now dead, executed by Herod Antipas.

The next pair of elements do speak of secondary witnesses to Jesus: John the Baptist (vv. 33–35, C) and the sacred Hebrew Scriptures (vv. 39–40, C′). Here Jesus censures his opponents on the grounds of their misplaced wills. They were *willing only for a time* to learn from John, and they were *not willing* to come to Jesus.

---

6. The "someone else" may refer to God (Kim, *Sourcebook*, 154) or the Baptist (Marsh, *Saint John*, 268-69).

7. The last time the Baptist is mentioned in this Gospel (10:40-41) is also in the past tense.

The crux of the paragraph is the parallel statement that the Father sent Jesus (vv. 36b–37; F, F′). It is the Father who gives his testimony that Jesus has come from God and acts with God's full authority.

A mini-chiasm closes the chapter. As is usual, the narrative closes with the key word "believe," but the concern here is the *absence* of faith. The religious leaders *cannot* believe in Jesus because they seek the praise of each other (v. 44, A), and *do not* believe in the written testimony of Moses (v. 47, A′). It is Moses, not Jesus, who will accuse them (vv. 45, 46; B, B′).

8

JOHN 6

Bread That Gives Life

THE CENTRAL SIGN OF the seven signs is the feeding of the large crowd. This story has many echoes of Israel's formative narrative, the exodus from Egypt. The backdrop is Passover time. A body of water is traversed. Food (manna, bread) is provided in a wilderness place. The people grumble. God's messenger goes up a mountain by himself.[1] We are faced with a new exodus. Other take-home theological lessons include Jesus' loving compassion, his unique relationship with the Creator God, and the symbolism of bread and eating for the eucharistic celebration.[2]

To start this chapter, two simple seven-part chiasms relate the stories that provide the basis for Jesus' subsequent teaching discourse. Jesus' teaching is presented in an extensive multi-part chiastic structure. This seems to be the first large chiasm that covers an extended conversation between Jesus and his religious detractors.[3] The chapter concludes with a description of how some disciples found Jesus' teaching unpalatable and so deserted him, a fourth chiasm.

1. Wright, *John, Part 1*, 72, 75; Ford, *Gospel of John*, 142.
2. Ford, *Gospel of John*, 143.
3. Large chiasms are found in 6:25–59 (as presented here), as well as chs. 7–8, 9, 11 (possibly), 17, and 18–19.

A Way of Reading John's Gospel

The first chiastic structure relates the feeding of the five thousand (fig. 17). Perhaps this and the next story manifest a chiastic structure only because that is the way dramatic stories develop and resolve. However, there is a general tendency for the centers of cruciform arrangements to express the punch line, often by presenting highly significant theological ideas, and the current stories could well be arranged to give prominence to these important teaching points.

¹ Setting: Jesus went across Lake Galilee (Lake Tiberias)

A ²⁻⁵ crowd followed, <u>had seen his signs</u> of healing; Jesus went up a <u>hill</u> with disciples; Passover Festival near; Jesus saw crowd <u>coming</u> to him
  B ^{5b-9} Jesus knew what he would do [human inadequacy]
  Philip: "Eight months wages would not buy enough bread"
  Andrew: "A boy, <u>five loaves of barley bread</u>, two fish, not enough"
    C ¹⁰ Jesus: "Make the people sit down," five thousand men
      D ¹¹ Jesus took the loaves, gave thanks, distributed the bread
      D' He did the same with the fish
    C' all had as much as they wanted
  B' ¹²⁻¹³ when all were full, "Gather the pieces left over;" filled twelve baskets with pieces from <u>five barley loaves</u> [divine abundance]
A' ¹⁴⁻¹⁵ <u>seeing this sign</u> that Jesus had performed, people said "This is the Prophet who was to come!" Jesus knew they were about to <u>come</u>, make him king by force, retired to the <u>hills</u> alone

Figure 17. Jesus Feeds a Large Crowd with Five Loaves and Two Fish (Sign 4, the Central One)

The first (vv. 2–5, A) element sets the scene and the last (vv. 14–15, A') concludes the action. They describe the setting of the event in the *hills* and the crowds who come to see Jesus' miraculous *signs*. In the final element, the people wondered if he is the Prophet (a leader anticipated by Moses, one who would be like Moses)[4] and they threatened to install him as king.

The second element (vv. 5b–9, B) describes human insufficiency. The people are out of food. The disciples do not have the resources to buy what is needed. All they can find is a boy's lunch: a paltry five barley loaves and some fish. The counterpart element

---

4. Deut 18:15 and 18:18–19, described in John 1:21 and 6:14 (above), and in 7:40; Wright, *John, Part 1*, 73, 107–8; Ford, *Gospel of John*, 144.

(vv. 12–13, B′) is all about the extravagance of divine provision. Those five barley loaves have been more than enough to feed the crowd.

The following pair of elements shows the magnitude of the problem, five thousand hungry men (v. 10, C), and the plenitude of God's response, five thousand satisfied men (v. 11b; C′).

The center describes how Jesus took the bread (v. 11a, D) and fish (v. 11a, D′), gave thanks, broke it, and distributed it. This is the closest John's Gospel comes to Jesus' enactment of the Lord's Supper, the new Passover, the sign of the new exodus. Together with the Last Supper and his action at Emmaus, it seems to represent an action that is characteristic of him.[5] Jesus gives thanks to God for the bread, representing his soon-to-be-broken body.

In our age, the family prayer of thanks before a meal is a daily reminder of God's sustaining care but is under threat of neglect. Perhaps this regular symbol should be emphasized as a continuous reminder of Jesus, the bread of life, no less important than the eucharistic celebration of the assembled *ekklesia*.

The second story relates how Jesus walked on the water to be with his disciples, who were struggling in the boat against adverse conditions (fig. 18). The first (vv. 16–17a, A) and last (vv. 22–24, A′) elements again provide the setting: the lake, boats, and the place to which they were heading, Capernaum. The second pair describes the initial difficulty of reaching the destination (vv. 17b–19a, B) and the final safe arrival there (v. 21b, B′) once Jesus was on board. This is followed by the parallel elements describing events in the boat: the disciples' first reaction of terror (v. 19b, C) and their glad relief as they welcome Jesus (v. 21a, C′).

---

5. Mark 14:22–25; Luke 24:30.

A ¹⁶⁻¹⁷ᵃ evening: Jesus' disciples to the <u>lake</u>, into a <u>boat</u>, back across the lake toward <u>Capernaum</u>
　B ¹⁷ᵇ⁻¹⁹ᵃ night: Jesus had not come to them, strong wind was blowing, stirring up the water; had rowed three or four miles
　　C ¹⁹ᵇ saw Jesus walking on water, coming <u>near the boat</u>, were terrified
　　　D ²⁰ Jesus: "Don't be afraid, it is I!"
　　C' ²¹ they gladly took him <u>into the boat</u>
　B' immediately the boat reached the destination
A' ²²⁻²⁴ next day: crowd, other side of the <u>lake</u>; there had been only one <u>boat</u> there, Jesus had not gone in it; <u>boats</u> from Tiberias came to the place where the crowd had eaten the bread; crowd saw that Jesus was not there, got into those <u>boats</u>, went to <u>Capernaum</u>, looking for him

Figure 18. Jesus Rules Creation[6]

The central element (v. 20, D) assures the disciples of Jesus' comfort, and follows this with the Gospel's second absolute "I am" statement.[7] Jesus identified himself as "It is I," but this could also be expressed as "I am." The person who feeds the hungry and rules over the stormy waters of creation, identifies himself with God by using the term "I am," the way by which God solemnly made his presence known to Israel.

The whole episode again places Jesus in the position of Israel's God. The Hebrew people had always been afraid of the sea. It represented chaos and the forces of evil. But YHWH ruled over it.[8] On this boisterous spring night, Jesus showed his control over it. He repudiated the notion of kingship as the excitable crowd understood it (vv. 14–15). But he demonstrates tacitly his genuine (divine) kingly authority by exercising his control over the watery chaos (v. 20, D).

Back in Capernaum, the crowd regathers. Their questioning elicits from Jesus an extended discourse on the bread that gives life (fig. 19). Like the Samaritan woman (ch. 4), the people are preoccupied with their physical needs, but Jesus directs the conversation to life as intimacy with God.

6. Jesus' second absolute "I am" statement is given (v. 20).

7. Bauckham, *Testimony*, 244–50.

8. Douglas et al., *Illustrated*, 1406–7; see Pss 77:16; 104:7–9; 148:7; Job 38:8–11; Acts 4:24.

JOHN 6

The first (v. 25, A) and last (v. 59, A') elements provide the context of the conversation, as is typical. Jesus is teaching in the synagogue. Interestingly, the black basalt rock foundations of what was probably a first century synagogue remain in Capernaum. The ruins of a fourth-century finely structured limestone synagogue are built upon the more roughly hewn basalt foundations of the earlier synagogue—probably the very venue in which Jesus taught.[9]

A 25 situation: Jesus, teacher, other side of the lake
  B 26-29 Jesus: do not work for <u>food</u> that spoils but that lasts for <u>eternal life</u>; believe in the one God <u>sent</u>
    C 30 people: What sign will you do that we may believe?
      D 31-33 Our <u>ancestors ate manna in the desert</u>, <u>bread from heaven</u>; Jesus: Truly, my Father gives <u>the true bread from heaven—he who comes down from heaven</u>, gives <u>life to the world</u>
        34 people: give us this <u>bread</u>
          E 35 Jesus: <u>I am the bread of life</u>
            F those <u>who come to me</u> will never be hungry; who <u>believe</u> in me will never be thirsty
              G 36-38 Everyone my Father gives me will come to me; I will never turn away anyone who comes to me; <u>I have come down from heaven</u> to do the will of him who sent me
                H 39 the <u>will</u> of him who sent me: I should not lose any, <u>raise them to life on the last day</u>
                  H' 40 Father's <u>will</u>: all who believe in the Son have eternal life; <u>I will raise them to life on the last day</u>
              G' 41-42 people grumble: <u>I am the bread that came down from heaven</u>? how can he say <u>he came down from heaven</u>?
            F' 43-47 Jesus: no one can <u>come to me</u> unless Father draws them; I will raise them to life on the last day; all who hear the Father <u>come to me</u>; who <u>believe</u> have eternal life
          E' 48 <u>I am the bread of life</u>
      D' 49-51 Your <u>ancestors ate manna in the desert</u>, died; whoever eats <u>the bread that comes down from heaven</u> will not die. I am the <u>living bread that came down from heaven</u>; eat this <u>bread</u>, <u>live</u> forever; the <u>bread</u> I give is my flesh, that the <u>world may live</u>
    C' 52 people: how can he give us his flesh to eat?
  B' 53 Jesus: unless you <u>eat the flesh of the Son of Man, drink his blood</u>, you will not have life
    54 <u>Those who eat my flesh, drink my blood</u> have <u>eternal life</u>; I will raise them to life on the last day
    55 my flesh is the true <u>food</u>; my blood the true drink
    56-57 <u>Those who eat my flesh, drink my blood</u> <u>live</u> in me, I <u>live</u> in them; the Father sent me, because of him I <u>live</u> also; whoever eats me will <u>live</u> because of me
    58 This is the bread that came down from heaven; not like the bread your ancestors ate but died, those who <u>eat this bread live forever</u>
A' 59 situation: Jesus, teaching, Capernaum synagogue

Figure 19. Jesus Is the Life-Giving Bread That Came from Heaven[10]

9. Evans, *Jesus and his World*, 31, 45–49.
10. The solemn claim that it is God's will that the Son should give eternal

The second (vv. 26-29, B) and penultimate (vv. 53-58, B′) elements directly transform the metaphor of eating bread (which sustains biological life) to the spiritual concept of feeding on (believing in) Jesus, the spiritual bread sent from God (which confers eternal life). Indeed, the notion of Jesus as the bread that gives eternal life is repeated in multiple parallel statements in the latter element (B′), which itself has features of a mini-chiasm. These two elements (B, B′) are connected by the term "food" (Greek, *brosis*, mentioned only in vv. 27 and 55). The crux of this mini-chiasm (v. 55) is that Jesus' flesh is the real food and his blood, the real drink. The breaking of Jesus' body and the spilling of his lifeblood, soon to happen on a Roman cross, represent the sacrifice of the Son by which humanity may be renewed. When people faithfully accept God's gift, they are infused with God's life.

The next pair of elements present the people's lack of understanding. First, they ask for a miracle, a sign (v. 30, C). Having heard of the story of how Jesus fed a large crowd, they are probably thinking of the repeat of a free lunch. In the parallel element, they ask how Jesus can give them his flesh to eat (v. 52, C′). Like the authorities in the temple, Nicodemus, and the Samaritan woman, they have been unable to understand Jesus' metaphors.

The next two elements of this discussion (vv. 31-34, D; vv. 49-51, D′) convey largely the same message. The Hebrew people who followed Moses in the Sinai desert ate manna ("bread from heaven"). But the Father gives the *real* bread from heaven—Jesus himself. He is the bread that comes down from heaven, that is life giving—indeed, that gives eternal life.[11] The second element progresses into the novel thought that the bread Jesus gives is his own flesh (v. 51).

The parallel pair (v. 35a, E; v. 48, E′) make the fundamental claim that Jesus is himself the bread of life—the first of the

---

life and raise his people on the last day is the central part of the central instance of the seven signs. This chiasm gives the first of Jesus' predicated "I am" (the bread of life) statements (vv. 35, 48).

11. That Jesus is the bread that has come down from heaven (D, D′, and v. 58, which serves as a summary statement in the extended B′ element), the one who has come down from heaven (G, G′) is integral to the chiasm.

predicated "I am" statements in John's Gospel. These elements are linked with those that describe the invitation that people should *come to* Jesus, *believe* in him, and so never hunger or thirst but have eternal life (v. 35b, F; vv. 43–47, F'). The next pair emphasizes that Jesus is the bread who has come down from heaven (vv. 36–38, G; v. 41, G').

The crux of the matter (v. 39, H; v. 40, H') is not the bread per se; it is the new life, the (current) eternal life and the (future) resurrection life that Jesus gives. The climax is given in directly parallel statements. It concerns the Father's express will or purpose.[12] And it states that Jesus is the one who gives effect to this will by raising to life on the last day the people who believe in him. This "raising to life on the last day" is repeated in vv. 44 and 54, representing a key development in the second half of the chiasm. John 6 is a resurrection chapter. John's Gospel describes eternal life as something received in the present—but makes it clear that its fullness is yet to come. The fullness awaits the resurrection on the last day. Wright, in considering the climax of this chapter, says, "The eternal life that begins in the present when someone believes, and continues in the future beyond death, will eventually take the form of the resurrection life."[13]

God's promised new age, the eschaton, has already been inaugurated, but it awaits completion. As theologians like to say, it is here already but not yet.

John 6 is an emotional roller-coaster. It describes Jesus' fourth sign and its comforting aftermath on the lake. This is followed by a forceful discussion in which Jesus presents himself as the life-giving bread—to the blank incomprehension of his interlocutors. And it concludes with the dispirited reaction of many of Jesus' followers to his teaching (again, his *logos*).[14] Jesus' challenge to his

---

12. The "purpose for which God created the universe" is to raise people from the dead, "to know him personally, and to talk with him and interact with him." Verney, *Water into Wine*, 86.
13. Wright, *John, Part 1*, 84.
14. John 6:60.

A Way of Reading John's Gospel

troubled and wavering followers is presented in chiastic form as depicted in figure 20.

```
A ⁶⁰ Many followers: "This teaching is too hard. Who can accept it?"
    B ⁶¹ Jesus knew that they were grumbling: "Does this make you want to give up?
        C ⁶² Suppose, that you see the Son of Man go back up to the place where he was before?
            D ⁶³ What gives life is God's Spirit; human power is impotent
               The words I have spoken bring God's life-giving Spirit.
                E ⁶⁴ some of you do not believe."
                  Jesus knew who would not believe, betray him
                    F ⁶⁵ "This is the reason I told you that no people can come to me
                    F' unless the Father makes it possible for them to do so."
                E' ⁶⁶ many of Jesus' followers turned back, would not go with him.
                   ⁶⁷ he asked the twelve: would you also like to leave?"
            D' ⁶⁸ Peter: Lord, to whom else should we go?
               You have the words that give eternal life.
        C' ⁶⁹ we believe and know that you are the Holy One, come from God"
    B' ⁷⁰ Jesus replied, "I chose the twelve of you? Yet one of you is a devil!"
A' ⁷¹ He was referring to Judas, son of Simon Iscariot, who was going to betray him.
```

Figure 20. The Life-Giving Father, Son, and Spirit

Many cannot bear Jesus' teaching (v. 60, A), and that seems to include Judas, whose perfidy is anticipated (v. 71, A'). Jesus knew of their grumbles (v. 61, B) and of the betrayer who lurked in his closest circle (v. 70, B').[15] Jesus challenged his disciples as to his divine origin with the Father (v. 62, C) and elicited Peter's confession that Jesus was the holy One, come from God (v. 69, C'). Peter's statement about believing provides the expected closure to the discourse.

Jesus asserts that his words communicate God's life-giving Spirit (v. 63, D), which Peter affirms (v. 68, D'). At the center of the pericope is a lament for those who *would not believe* (v. 64, E) and *would not go* with him (vv. 66–67, E'). The crux of the matter is that anyone who comes to Jesus does so not by their own innate abilities (v. 65a, F) but by a work of the Father himself (v. 65b, F'). This is a spiritual work, not one that people can do by their own ingenuity or effort. There is no occasion for pride—a challenge to the mindset of our narcissistic age.

---

15. Where most translations render v. 70 "one of you is a devil," an alternative might be "one of you is an accuser"—a prescient description of Judas's action. Wright, *John, Part 1*, 92.

9

JOHN 7–8

Festival of Shelters Disputation

THESE TWO CHAPTERS ARE one unit, and the chapter boundary is misleading because it obscures the unity of the two chapters. The location of the action is in the temple, the very heart of Israel's life. The occasion is the important week-long Festival of Shelters (or of Tabernacles).[1] This annual festival celebrates both the completed harvest and the journey of the Hebrews under Moses' leadership through the desert. For the latter reason the people celebrating the festival lived for a week in temporary shelters made out of branches and palm leaves.[2] In John's Gospel, the events at the Festival of Shelters, described in 7:1—10:21, point to the incarnation of Jesus, who "*tabernacled* among us" (1:14).[3]

After the return from Babylon, the celebration included a ceremony of water pouring, which was not prescribed in the Hebrew Scriptures. Water from the pool of Siloam, just below the temple, was collected in a golden vessel and poured out over the altar as an act of worship.[4] This ritual recognized rain as a gift of God, a

---

1. In Hebrew, Succoth; it is also called the Feast of Booths.
2. Lev 23:39–43.
3. Marsh, *Saint John*, 327.
4. Phillips, "Pools of Siloam," 45–46.

precondition for good harvests.⁵ It was also a reminder of the water that gushed out of a rock during the desert migration. Another feature of the festival was the lighting of four golden candlesticks as night descended at the close of the first day of the festival. The blaze of light was seen throughout Jerusalem and was an occasion of unrestrained joy.⁶

Chapter 7 commences with an exchange between Jesus and his unbelieving brothers as to when Jesus would travel to Jerusalem for the festival. Jesus recognized that he was a marked man. It seemed to be general knowledge that the authorities wanted to kill him (7:1, 11). He traveled to Jerusalem belatedly and secretly. An introductory comment sets the scene (7:10–13).

THE IDENTITY OF JESUS

A large chiastic structure unites both chapters (fig. 21). The chiastic unit begins with Jesus teaching in the temple to the surprise of the authorities, who are impressed with his teaching (7:14–15, A and B). The narrative finishes with the authorities again showing surprise (if not outraged incredulity) when Jesus claims, "Before Abraham was born, 'I am'" (8:58). This is the fifth absolute "I am" statement and Jesus was unambiguously claiming divine identity.⁷ The violently angry reaction of the authorities demonstrates that Jesus' assertion should be understood in this way. The curtain to the drama falls as Jesus hides himself and escapes from the temple (8:56–59, B', A').

---

5. Douglas et al., *Illustrated*, 1512.
6. Barclay, *Gospel of John*, 2:12.
7. Bauckham, *Testimony*, 245.

JOHN 7-8

Figure 21. Controversy at the Festival of Shelters: Who Is This Man?[8]

The third (7:16–18, C) and third-from-last (8:54–55, C') elements focus on the relationship between Jesus and his Father. Jesus

---

8. This dialogue includes the Gospel's second "I am" statement with the predicate "the light of the world" (8:12), the third, fourth, and fifth absolute "I am" statements (8:24, 28, 58). The words *ego eimi* are given as "I Am Who I Am" (vv. 24, 28) in the GNT and JBP (though it is expressed as "I am who I say I am" in v. 28 JBP); it is translated as "I am he" in the RSV, the NIV gives the alternative "I am," and the JB reads, "I am He." The suggestion that the water that Jesus gives is the Spirit (see John 4) is here made explicit. The story of the woman charged with adultery is found at the point indicated by an asterisk.

sought to give glory to the Father and was truthful in what he said. And the Father honored Jesus, who knew him and obeyed him.

In the fourth and fourth-from-last elements, Jesus referred to the two greatest figures in Israel's history. First he cited Moses, the leader who led the exodus from Egypt, and who subsequently delivered Israel's Law, the Torah. Jesus charged the authorities with disobeying Moses' law. They should *do* the law Moses gave (7:19–23, D). Then he referred to Abraham, the revered ancestor of Israel and the paradigm of obedient faith. Jesus said that the people should *do* the things Abraham did and alleged that they were deserting Abraham for the father of lies (8:33–53, D'). Both elements indicate that these stern words were given because of the people's plan to kill Jesus. Their angry response was to assert that Jesus was demon possessed.

In these fourth and fourth-from-last elements, Jesus appealed to the people. Judge by true, right standards (7:24, D). Recognize the God-given mission of Jesus, so as to know the truth and be set free (8:31–32, D'). Perhaps the issue at stake was that the people should rejoice that a crippled man had been healed and given the gift of *shalom*, wholeness (7:21; cf. ch. 5)—and so judge righteously, and come to know the truth. They should not cavil because their misconstrued ideas about Sabbath observance had been contravened.[9]

The issues of Jesus' death and identity then arose. First the people asked whether Jesus was the man who the authorities wanted to kill and whether he could be the Messiah (7:25–26, E). In the parallel element, Jesus stated how he would be killed. He would be "lifted up" (an ambivalent phrase referring to both crucifixion and glorification) and this would establish his identity as "I am," the fourth absolute "I am" statement (8:27–30, E'). The GNT translates this as "I am who I am," the divine name revealed to Moses at the burning bush.[10]

The following pair of elements (7:27–36, F; 8:14–26, F') continues Jesus' dialogue with the people, and they are similar in

---

9. Marsh, *Saint John*, 333–34.
10. Exod 3:14.

content. There was controversy over where this man (Jesus) came from. The One who sent Jesus is truthful. The people did not know the Father, the one who sent him. Nor did they know Jesus. Jesus would go away, but the people could not go where Jesus was going. The issue of *believing* in Jesus also came up—but comprised the major difference between the pair of elements. In the former element, many people's faith led them to ask if Jesus was the Messiah (7:31). In the latter, Jesus spoke of the requirement that people should believe in his absolute "I am" self-designation (8:24)—the claim to deity, the third instance of this in John's Gospel. The authorities met this claim with evident incomprehension (v. 25). John's Gospel represents *believing* in different degrees. People might believe in Jesus as Messiah, but this is inadequate. They needed to progress to a faith in Jesus as one who shares in the identity of Israel's God YHWH.

The following pair of statements are profoundly important proclamations of Jesus. Taking his cue from the water-pouring ceremony, Jesus invited thirsty people to come to him and drink (7:37-39, G). Jesus appropriated to himself the gushing, life-giving spring that sustained the Hebrew people during their journey through the desert. He echoed what YHWH had said to Israel: "Come all you who are thirsty, come to the waters."[11] This provoked a flurry of controversy.[12]

The paired invitation arose out of the dramatic light-in-the-darkness feature of the festival, the evocative chiaroscuro effect of the great candles burning at night. "I am the light of the world. Whoever follows me will have the light of life" (8:12-13, G'). This is the second predicated "I am" statement in the Gospel. Again, Jesus claimed for himself what the Hebrew Scriptures attributed to YHWH: "The Lord [YHWH] is my light and my salvation."[13] Marsh has said, "The world for man is a dark and mysterious place;

---

11. Isa 55:1-3. To Jews, this pronouncement had echoes of Ezek 47:1-12; to Christians, in the light of the resurrection, of Rev 21:6 and 22:1-2. Ford, *Gospel of John*, 170.

12. Bailey, *Jesus*, 231.

13. Ps 27:1; Isa 60:19-20.

human life, its origin, its course, and its destiny, is shrouded in mystery; Jesus in his coming has brought divine light to play upon the darkness and has shown man the reality of his situation in a final and authoritative act of illumination."[14]

Sandwiched between Jesus' great statements is controversy. The crowd argued among themselves (7:40–44, H), as did the religious leaders with one of their own, Nicodemus (vv. 50–53, H'), over whether the Messiah could come from Galilee. The leaders argue with the guards as to why they did not arrest Jesus (7:45, I; vv. 47–49, I'). At the center of the entire dialogue is the guards' confession: "Nobody ever talked the way this man does" (7:46, J). Is this apparently mild confession an anticlimax to the dialogue? Perhaps not: here we have a group of men who are not Jesus' sympathizers, as John the Baptist had been, giving their testimony to Jesus' authority. The guards were responsible for protecting the temple. And yet when asked why they had not obeyed orders, they told the assembled teachers and leaders of Israel that they were not in the same league as this provincial rabbi. Jesus' words are truthful; they are unique.

The second half of the chiasm introduces a major theological point, as observed in other instances. Despite the symmetry of form, it is only late in the text that Jesus describes himself as "I am"—three times (8:24, 28, 58). Here is a concentration of three of the absolute "I am" sayings.[15] This term would have an unmistakable association with the self-designation of God in the Hebrew Scriptures. Jesus "speaks of himself in a way that recalls the Old Testament's way of speaking about God."[16] It is a claim to divinity. It provoked his hearers into picking up stones.[17] The discussion seems to conclude abruptly.

---

14. Marsh, *Saint John*, 353.
15. Bauckham, *Testimony*, 244.
16. Wenham and Walton, *Exploring*, 261.
17. The first of a sequence of occasions in which Jesus was said to be threatened with stoning, starting at 8:59, 10:31, and 11:8.

JOHN 7-8

TEST CASE: THE MEANING OF MOSES' LAW

I have overlooked the story commonly known as "the woman taken in adultery" (John 7:53—8:11).[18] Its location at this point tends to obscure the obvious chiastic structure that spans chapters 7 and 8,[19] and it had to be bracketed out to facilitate analysis of that chiasm. This story is absent from many old manuscripts, and occurs at a variety of places when it is present.[20]

Some scholars question its authenticity.[21] Most scholars support the idea that "the passage is an interpolation into the Gospel of John."[22] Perhaps it is located at the start of chapter 8 in our Bibles because it shares the theme of the debate reported in chapters 7 and 8 in which Jesus denounced the hard-heartedness of the religious leaders. The story could be linked with Jesus' statement that the authorities make judgments according to purely human criteria whereas he (Jesus) passes judgment on no one (8:15). The story describes how the authorities suggested that the woman be stoned (8:5); the debate in the temple concludes with the desire of the authorities that Jesus be stoned (8:59).[23]

Another alternative is that the story was originally present at this place in the text but was deleted by many copyists because they were afraid that the mercy shown by Jesus might encourage laxity in sexual behavior. The story "violated deeply rooted cultural attitudes."[24] And this would not be the only time in John's

---

18. Wright, *John, Part 1*, 111; Wright and Bird suggest that the story may be better entitled "the men caught in hypocrisy." See Wright and Bird, *New Testament*, 669.

19. At least one scholar has noted that the pericope disrupts the flow of chapters 7–8 (without alluding to the chiastic structure). Daniel B. Wallace writes that the passage "seriously disrupts the flow of the argument." Wallace, "Gospel of John," §52, quoted in Grabiner, "Pericope Adulterae," 98.

20. Indeed, the first verse after the story of the adulterous woman (8:12) is probably linked directly with the last verse before this story (7:52) by the words "*Again* Jesus spoke." Kim, *Sourcebook*, 234n4, (italics added).

21. See, for example, Evans, *Jesus*, 80.

22. Grabiner, "Pericope Adulterae," 93.

23. Wright, *John, Part 1*, 112.

24. Bailey, *Jesus*, 230.

A Way of Reading John's Gospel

Gospel when Jesus urges someone, "Do not sin again" (here, in 8:11; see also 5:14).[25]

Nevertheless, this story itself is composed as a chiastic structure.[26] As such, it is typical of what we have seen in John's Gospel (fig. 22). The first and final elements bracket the story. The prosecutors appear with the accused person against whom a charge is to be made (v. 3a, A). But when the pericope reaches its conclusion, the prosecutors have absented themselves, the charge has been dropped, and the accused has been freed (vv. 10–11, A′). Jesus expresses his unconditional forgiveness of the woman, based solely on his authority—another pointer to his superiority over Moses and to his divine status.[27]

7:53—8:2 Jesus went to the Mount of Olives; next morning, back to the Temple; people gathered, he sat down, began to teach

A ³ teachers of the Law, Pharisees brought a woman, caught committing adultery
 B they made her stand before them all
  C ⁴⁻⁶ they said to Jesus: "Teacher, this woman was caught in the act of adultery; Moses commanded that such a woman be stoned; what do you say?"—to trap, accuse Jesus
   D he bent over and wrote on the ground with his finger
    E ⁷ they stood asking him questions
    E he stood up: "The one without sin may throw the first stone"
   D ⁸ he bent over again and wrote on the ground
  C ⁹ When they heard this, they left, one by one, older ones first
 B Jesus was left alone with the woman still [standing] there
A ¹⁰⁻¹¹ He stood up: "Where are they? no one left to condemn you?" woman: "No one, sir;" Jesus: "I do not condemn you. Go, do not sin again"

Figure 22. Jesus Challenges an Adulterous Woman and Self-Righteous Men

The second element (v. 3b, B) sees the victim paraded in humiliation before everyone. It is an acutely embarrassing scene. But in the penultimate element (v. 9b, B′), the awkwardness, the shame, and the public censure have dissipated. It is a tender scene

---

25. See John 5:14. In the Greek, *mekete hamartane*.

26. According to Kim, it is acknowledged that this story has a general chiastic structure, ABB′A′. Kim, *Sourcebook*, 235–37.

27. Burge, "Specific Problem," 145, quoted in Grabiner, "*Pericope Adulterae*," 93.

as Jesus stands alone with the woman, her accusers having slunk away. Both elements place the drama amid (Greek, *en meso*) the crowd of onlookers.[28] Much was at stake in this showdown.

The central part of the chiasm features Jesus and the prosecutors. They state the charge and suggest a harsh penalty (vv. 4–6a, C). The scenario is a trick. Would Jesus say, "Let her go" (and so set aside the Law of Moses) or "Stone her" (and so set aside the law of Rome)? Following Jesus' response and, one might imagine, an agonizing silence, they slip away. The most senior go first (v. 9a, C′) presumably because they would have been the ones expected to initiate proceedings.[29] The guilt, the shame, and the opprobrium have been transferred on to them. The rigid defenders of Torah have been vanquished. They know that all people are condemned before the bar of God's holiness.

Jesus has created tension of his own by writing (who knows what) on the ground using his finger (v. 6b, D; v. 8, D′).[30] And his bombshell judgment, which is delivered at the center of the chiasm, is to say that the person without sin may initiate the execution (v. 7, E). It appears that the heinousness of the sin of self-righteousness is the main teaching point of this story. We know that we all stand convicted before God. But there is mercy for all.

---

28. Ford, *Gospel of John*, 176.

29. Marsh, *Saint John*, 687.

30. The law of Moses was "written with the finger of God" (Exod 31:18). When Jesus wrote with his finger, was he implying, here is the true law, or even, here is the true lawgiver?

10

JOHN 9

Lord of the Sabbath II: Opposing Spiritual Blindness

JESUS WAS AGAIN IN Jerusalem where he performed another sign—the fifth in the Gospel and a pair with the third sign (the healing of the paralysed man at the pool of Bethzatha). This story features the pool of Siloam, a landmark of pre-AD 70 Jerusalem rediscovered by workmen repairing an underground pipe in June 2004.[1] Archaeological exploration is continuing in 2023. We are informed that the Hebrew word *Siloam* means "sent" (9:7). As the water from the spring of Gihon was *sent* to the pool of Siloam, so it is thematic in John's Gospel that the Father has *sent* Jesus into the world.[2]

The entirety of chapter 9 appears to be structured chiastically as a single unit. It uses a case of physical blindness to highlight the prevalence of spiritual blindness among the Jewish authorities (fig. 23). It is thus a sequel of the controversy reported in chapters 7 and 8.

---

1. Phillips, "Pools of Siloam," 41; "Ancient Siloam Pool," para. 7.
2. Phillips, "Pools of Siloam," 52; see John 5:30–40; 6:38–58; 7:16–34; 8:12–30, 42; 10:36; 11:42; 12:44–49.

JOHN 9

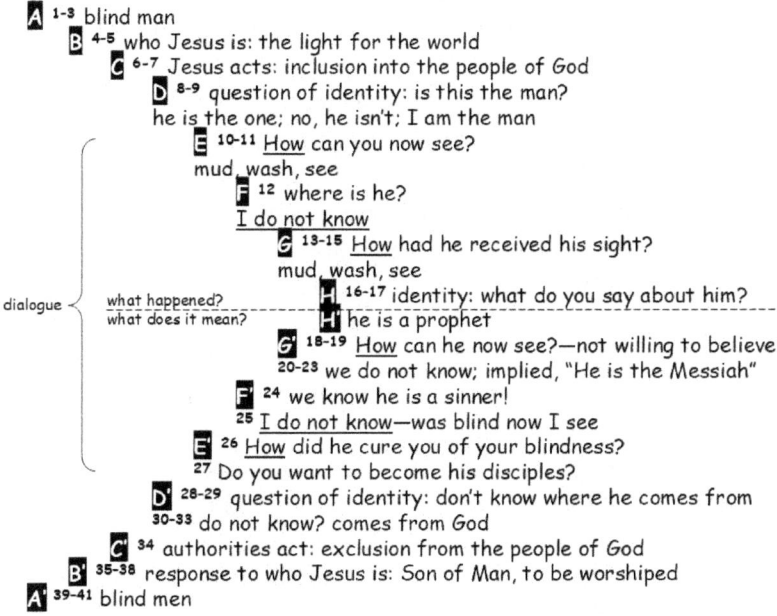

Figure 23. Sabbath Healing at Siloam (Sign 5)

The first (vv. 1–3, A) and final (vv. 39–41, A′) elements are concerned with blindness. We are introduced to a man who was born blind. Jesus makes it clear that random misfortune should not be seen as an act of divine judgment.[3] All people are subject to happenstance, but good can come out of tragedy when people respond in faith and obedience. The episode concludes with Jesus' assertion that the religious leaders were in fact spiritually blind. Jesus' mission was to bring spiritual insight to those who lacked it, and to show that those who (claimed they could) see were to be adjudged as in fact (spiritually) blind. Marsh indicates that *seeing* could be used in the sense of *believing*; and *being blind* in the sense of *not believing*. The religious leaders professed to *know*, to *see*. Jesus effectively told them that "your blindness is not an affliction for which you cannot be blamed, but an act of refusal for which

---

3. As is made clear also in Luke 13:1–5.

71

you must accept responsibility."[4] Blindness itself is not an indication of sin, but claiming to be able to see when you cannot see certainly is [5]

The second (vv.4–5, B) and penultimate (vv. 35–38, B′) elements focus on the identity of Jesus himself. He provides a repeat of his claim to be the light of the world (a link with the discussion at the Festival of Shelters, 8:12). The healing story culminates in the once-blind man kneeling before Jesus as the Son of Man,[6] and affirming his faith in him: "I believe Lord" (v. 38).

The next parallel pair contrasts the effect of Jesus' and the authorities' actions. The healing story is given in two brief verses (vv. 6–7, C). Jesus acted to restore the man's sight, and so to *restore him into* the fellowship of Israel. Some Jews (at least) regarded people with physical defects, such as blindness, as being blemished and less than fully Israelite. Jesus' sign restored the gift of *shalom* (wholeness), which included full membership in Israel.[7] In their pique, the authorities acted to expel the man from the synagogue. They *excluded him from* the fellowship of Israel (v. 34, C′).

The fourth element from each end is concerned with the issue of *identity*. First, there is uncertainty over the identity of the man who was healed (vv. 8–9, D). Second, the man who was healed affirmed the identity of Jesus: this man who restored his sight has come from God (vv. 28–33, D′), a theme that has surfaced repeatedly already. Jesus must be doing what God wants him to do.

Once again, despite the symmetry of form, there is a notable development of theological teaching through the story. Whereas the first half is about the evidence for the healing (what happened?), the second half describes a debate about the identity of Jesus (what does it mean?). The question "How?" is asked four times in the conversation. In the first two elements, the question

---

4. Marsh, *Saint John*, 390.

5. Wright, *John, Part 1*, 144.

6. Wright, *John, Part 1*, 145; considered here to reflect the figure from the prophecy of Dan 7:13–14, "who is exalted to a seat alongside God and given the task of bringing God's judgment to the world."

7. Wright, *Jesus*, 191–92.

and the answer given pertain to the events that transpired (vv. 10–11, E; vv. 13–15, G). In the latter two cases (vv. 26–27, E'; vv. 18–23, G', parallels of the first two), the issue raised is about the nature of Jesus himself. Should people be his disciples (v. 27)? Is he the Messiah (v. 22)?

The central element asks the key question in the most direct form: What do you say about *him*? (vv. 16–17a, H), and offers a tentative answer: He is a prophet (v. 17b, H'). This title might seem a little underwhelming relative to some of the other designations applied to Jesus. Wright makes the point that New Testament writings apart from the Gospels did not feature Jesus as a prophet. However, the Gospels preserve a historically situated understanding of Jesus. He was a prophet, like those of the Hebrew Scriptures, "coming to Israel with a word from her covenant god, warning her of the imminent and fearful consequences of the direction she was traveling, urging and summoning her to a new and different way."[8] Jesus had a prophetic role just like (say) Jeremiah, even if, as the Gospels make clear, he was more than a prophet.

---

8. Wright, *Jesus*, 163; see also 162–68.

11

JOHN 10

Jesus Is the Good Shepherd

THE CONTROVERSY BETWEEN JESUS and the Jewish authorities, as described in 7:10—9:41, flows into the current chapter.[1] Who is the true leader of the people, the flock of Israel? Jesus presents the parable of the sheep and the good shepherd, and he makes it clear that he is that good shepherd. He identifies the authorities as being usurpers who do not have the best interests of the flock at heart, although he is not explicit about this identification. The authorities are like thieves and robbers or, at best, hired people who act as shepherds merely as a source of income.

Verses 1–18 appear to form a chiasm with some noteworthy features (fig. 24). The first (vv. 1–4, A) and final (vv. 16–18, A′) elements include the main components of Jesus' figure of speech: the sheep pen, the shepherd (who, as indicated below, is Jesus) and the sheep (which are defined by their responsiveness to the shepherd's

---

1. Marsh, *Saint John*, 393; Ford, *Gospel of John*, 203.

voice).² The sheep represent the people whom Jesus has come to save: Israel, "worried and helpless, like sheep without a shepherd."³

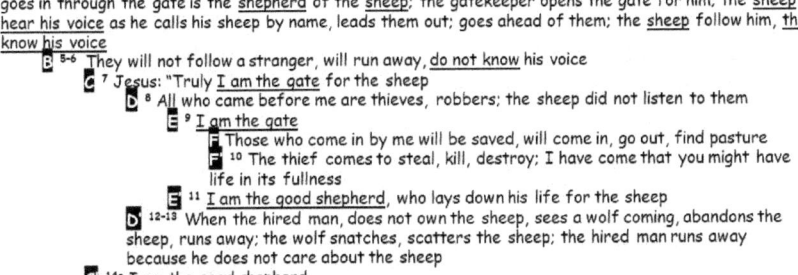

Figure 24. The Metaphor of the Sheep and the Shepherd⁴

There are also concepts specific to each element. In the first one, the idea of thieves and robbers is raised, with an eye to the authorities who expelled the formerly blind man from the synagogue. In the last one, Jesus speaks of sheep that have not belonged to this sheep pen—probably Samaritans and gentiles, "that great company, from every nation under heaven, that God intends to save, and to save through Jesus."⁵ Such people are destined to become one flock with Israel. Jesus also speaks of willingly giving

---

2. Perhaps both elements also feature the Father, explicitly in the final element (vv. 17, 18) and implicitly in v. 3: is it possible that the gatekeeper represents the Father, the one under whose loving and discerning eye the sheep are welcomed into the sheep pen?

3. Matt 9:36.

4. This section contains two more "I am" clauses with predicates (numbers 3 and 4): Jesus identifies himself as the gate (v. 7, C; v. 9, E) and, in parallel elements to these, as the good shepherd (v. 11, E'; vv. 14–15, C').

5. Wright, *John, Part 1*, 152.

his own life—an idea developed earlier in the second half of the chiasm. Once again, although there is symmetry of chiastic structure, novel aspects of content have appeared in the second half of the chiasm.

The next pair of elements (vv. 5–6, B; vv. 14b–15, B′) share in common the theme that the sheep and the true shepherd *know* each other. The second statement develops the idea that the Father and Son know each other in the same way as the shepherd and sheep know each other. Ford describes how this knowing gives the reader scope for unlimited reflection: the Father knows Jesus "by name; in utter love and wisdom; with joy and delight; with complete understanding."[6] And this intimacy is a model of the sheep's knowledge of the shepherd—except of course that the sheep are learners that need to grow in this knowledge. Moreover, the shepherd is willing to lay down his life in sacrifice for the sheep (v. 15b).

In the next pair of elements, Jesus identifies himself as the gate (v. 7, C) and the good shepherd (v. 14a, C′). This apparent mixing of metaphors cannot be an accident because a subsequent gate claim (v. 9a, E) is again paired with a subsequent shepherd claim (v. 11, E′). And yet the two terms may not be far apart. According to scholars, in the towns the sheep pen had a gate, controlled by the doorkeeper. But in the countryside, the sheep pen had an opening through which the sheep freely moved. At night, the shepherd lay across that opening, so no sheep (or predator) could enter or leave without walking over his body. The shepherd was in fact the gate, so that "through him alone men find access to God."[7]

To call oneself the good shepherd is a provocative assertion. The Hebrew Scriptures were emphatic that YHWH was the true Shepherd of Israel. "As a shepherd looks after his scattered flock when he is with then, so I will look after my sheep. I will rescue them[,] ... gather them[,] ... pasture them[,] ... tend them[,] ... shepherd the flock with justice."[8] Jesus here indicates that he fulfils

---

6. Ford, *Gospel of John*, 209–10.
7. Barclay, *Gospel of John*, 2:67; Wright, *John, Part 1*, 150.
8. Ezek 34: 11–16; see also Ps 23.

the shepherd role that rightly and exclusively belongs to YHWH. Jesus fulfils a role that is God's alone.

Each identification of Jesus as the good shepherd includes the idea that Jesus is willing to die for the sheep (vv. 11, 15b, vv. 17–18, five times overall in the second half of this section). The thief exploits the sheep (v. 8, D). The hired man deserts them in the face of danger (vv. 12–13, D′). These are images of the selfish religious leaders. But the real shepherd gives his life in sacrifice for them.

The parallel sentences at the center speak of the salvation of the sheep. They will be saved and find pasture (v. 9b, F). To "go in and come out" is Hebrew idiom that intimates one may live unmolested, in absolute security.[9] And they will have life in all its fullness (v. 10, F′). At this point, the metaphor changes from Jesus the gate ("those who come in by me") to Jesus the shepherd (unlike the thief, Jesus has come to give life). And the sheep's *living* (v. 10) is connected with the sheep's *knowing* (vv. 5, 15) as will be shown later.[10]

The pericope finishes with a summary of the people's reaction to Jesus' words. There is a heated exchange between them. Many considered Jesus to be demon possessed or mad. Some recognized Jesus' fifth sign, the Sabbath healing at Siloam, as authenticating his divine commission.

The debate continued in Jerusalem, in the temple, but in a different setting. This one was the joyous festival of the dedication of the temple, Hanukkah. It celebrated the purification of the temple in 164 BC by Judas Maccabeus, after it had been desecrated by the Greek king Antiochus Epiphanes. But in John's Gospel, Jesus' words at Hanukkah point to the replacement of Herod's Temple building on Mount Zion by the new temple who was to be Jesus himself: "the one meeting place of God and man."[11] On the day when the dedication (sanctification) of the temple was celebrated, Jesus stated that the Father chose ("sanctified," v. 36) him and sent him into the world.[12]

9. Barclay, *Gospel of John*, 2:68.
10. See 10:27–28 below, and the Lord's high priestly prayer, John 17:3.
11. Marsh, *Saint John*, 403.
12. Ford, *Gospel of John*, 211, 213.

A Way of Reading John's Gospel

Jesus' teaching and debating do not seem to be presented as an obvious chiasm. However, there are some features that hint at a cruciform structure (fig. 25). The first element describes the people's impatient demand to be told whether Jesus identified himself as the Messiah (v. 24, A). But by the conclusion of the discussion, they had become aware of Jesus' claim to unity with the Father, and they were incensed by it (v. 39, A′).

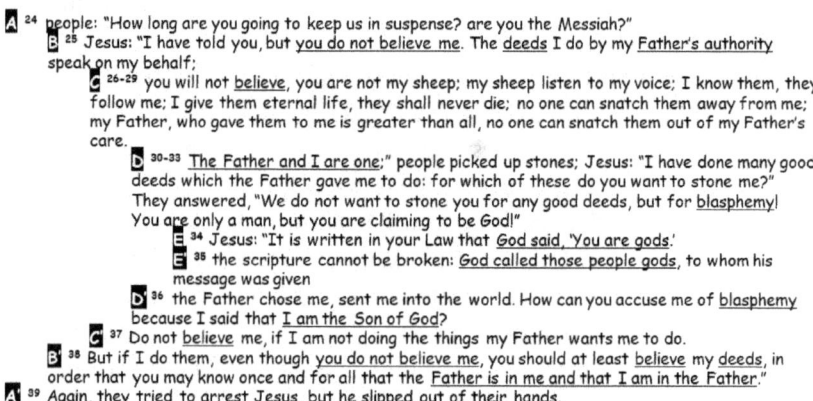

Figure 25. Jesus Teaches: Festival of the Dedication of the Temple[13]

In the next pair of elements, Jesus chided the people who did not *believe* him (v. 25, B; v. 38, B′). This disbelief was blameworthy because of the *deeds* that Jesus had done—the signs such as the healing of the blind man described in chapter 9 at, or soon after, the Festival of Shelters. Jesus' deeds were done by the Father's authority, the Father and Son being in intimate fellowship.

The third and third-to-last elements further deal with reasons for disbelief. The people did not believe in Jesus because they were not his sheep (vv. 26–29, C). This is despite what Jesus has done for the sheep. He calls them, knows them, leads them, gives

---

13. In v. 29, the sense given is found in the JB, JBP, NIV, and RSV translations; cf. GNT: "What my Father has given me is greater than everything."

them eternal life, and keeps them safe. The only reason for disbelief—that is, for rejecting Jesus—would be if he was not carrying out his Father's commission (v. 37, C'). That is, they do not believe because they do not recognise Jesus' actions as doing the Father's work.

In the fourth elements, the stakes are further raised. Jesus went beyond his deeds (done in obedience to the Father) to assert the intimacy of his relationship with his Father. "The Father and I are one" provokes the charge of blasphemy (vv. 30–33, D). The people alleged that Jesus had impugned God's honor. But Jesus rejected the charge of blasphemy by reiterating that God chose him and sent him into the world. And he doubled down on his claim by stating that he was the Son of God (v. 36, D').

What did Jesus mean by stating that he and the Father were one? The answer may be found in Jesus' prayer to the Father in which Jesus prayed that the disciples would be one as "we [Father and Son] are one."[14] This oneness referred to intimacy of relationship, and depended on love, which was itself to be manifested in the disciples' unity with each other.[15] In its immediate context, Jesus' comment could simply mean that he and the Father were "united in purpose and agency."[16] But the religious leaders could have been serving the author's intentions by interpreting Jesus' statement as a claim to divinity. It has been suggested (not necessarily in contradistinction to the idea of intimacy discussed above) that Jesus was here referring to the great Jewish affirmation of faith, the Shema: "The Lord our God is one Lord."[17] If this were true, Jesus would be including himself in the identity of YHWH, the one God.[18]

Jesus legitimized his extraordinary claim by appealing to the Hebrew Scriptures (vv. 34–35; E, E'). He cites unchangeable spiritual truth as it is believed to reside in Scripture, using a rabbinic

14. John 17:11, 21–23.
15. Barclay, *Gospel of John*, 2:86–87.
16. Ford, *Gospel of John*, 213.
17. Deut 6:4.
18. Bauckham, *Testimony*, 250–51.

A Way of Reading John's Gospel

strategy of exegesis. (Yes, it sounds very strange to us.) He cites the ancient text in which the judges of Israel were addressed by God as gods, *elohim*.[19] They were commissioned to bring God's justice and help to their fellow Israelites. They represented God to human beings. They were effectively God to people. The analogy is that Jesus claimed that he had a special commission to communicate God's message to humanity. He truly represented the Father to human beings. He was God to them.[20]

The chiasm is followed by the expected statement regarding people's *believing* (vv. 40–42). After this time of deepening conflict, Jesus retreated to the place where John had baptized him, where his commission had been given. Even he needed to reflect again on the Father's call. And despite the tension and rejection, the episode concludes with the comment that there were many who did believe in him.

---

19. Ps 82:6. Other texts in the Jewish law also described the judges as gods (Exod 21:6; 22:9, 28); see Barclay, *Gospel of John*, 2:88–89.

20. This style of argumentation has been said to be compelling to Jesus' Jewish hearers, even though it does not work for us. After all, the human judges of Israel were gods only in a metaphorical sense; Jesus is claiming to be the Son of the Father in actual reality. Perhaps this is an argument *from the lesser to the greater*: if the holy Scriptures could describe fallible human judges as gods, *how much more* could we see the fully obedient Son as God. See Ford, *Gospel of John*, 214.

12

JOHN 11

Jesus Is the Resurrection

THE NARRATIVE OF THE raising of Lazarus is told in chiastic form that occupies nearly all of chapter 11 (fig. 26). It starts with an introductory comment that situated Lazarus and his family in the history of Jesus (vv. 1–2). Thereafter the narrative develops with chiastic character. Jesus and his disciples heard news that Lazarus was sick. There was a delay before the decision was made to return to Judea (vv. 3–7, A). The story concludes with Jesus and his disciples hiding as fugitives in Judea before their retreat to a lonely place called Ephraim (v. 54, A').

In the second and second-to-last elements, the underlying dangers are raised. The disciples acknowledged that Jesus has enemies in Judea who would like to stone him (vv. 8–10, B). Jesus assured them that to do God's bidding—to walk in the light—is the most secure place to be. The authorities' nefarious scheming was laid bare at the end of the narrative: Jesus was seen to be a troublemaker and (according to Caiaphas, the high priest) it was better to eliminate Jesus than to run the risk of having social disorder that could lead to Roman military action (vv. 46–53, B').[1] With

---

1. This is the only time in any of the Gospels that the Romans are explicitly mentioned. But it grounds the story of Jesus firmly in historical reality, as popular revolts had led to cruel and devastating Roman repression both a few

profound irony, Caiaphas opined that it was preferable that one man should die for the people. His logic reflected corrupt political expediency, but at the level of God's holy purposes, Caiaphas had stated exactly what Jesus' death would accomplish. Jesus' walking in the light would entail his death on behalf of Jew and gentile.

Jesus spoke of his purpose to wake Lazarus from the sleep of death (vv. 11–13, C), and he brought that purpose to actuality (vv. 43–45, C′). Jesus stated—both before setting out for Bethany (vv. 14–16, D) and when he had arrived at the tomb (vv. 40–42, D′)—that the outcome of this crisis was that people would come to *believe* in him. The situation according to all present was hopeless, as Lazarus had been dead for four days (v. 17, E; vv. 38b–39, E′). The poignancy of the situation is portrayed, both as it affected the crowd of comforters (vv. 18–19, F) and Jesus himself, who was "deeply moved" and who wept (vv. 33–38a, F′). God present in the Messiah surely shares our griefs.

The next elements are strongly paralleled. Martha's (vv. 20–21, G) and Mary's (vv. 28–32, G′) responses to Jesus are given in the same terms. The sisters separately went out to meet him. And they offered the same impressive but (to the writer) inadequate degree of faith: "If you had been here, Lord, my brother would not have died!" Yes, they had faith but perhaps John (with his penchant for irony) wanted to show that it was too modest and would soon be jolted into a new plane.

The following elements reveal Martha's developing faith. She uttered several creedal affirmations. She expressed confidence that God would answer Jesus' requests and that the dead would rise in the final resurrection (vv. 22–24, H). And she confessed that Jesus was the Messiah (v. 27, H′).[2] This was commendable faith but would be shown to be relativized by what was to follow.

---

decades before and after Jesus' mission. Wright, *John, Part 2*, 17–19.

2. She confessed in the same unambiguous terms as Peter used (albeit more frequently cited); see Mark 8:29, Matt 16:16, and Luke 9:20.

JOHN 11

¹⁻² Lazarus, sick in Bethany, where Mary, Martha lived
(Mary poured perfume on the Lord's feet, wiped them with her hair)

A ³⁻⁷ sisters: "Lord, the man you love is sick." Jesus: "This sickness will bring glory to God, Son of God" Jesus loved Martha, her sister, Lazarus; stayed where he was for two more days; Jesus to disciples, "Let us go back to Judea"
  B ⁸⁻¹⁰ disciples: "Teacher, the people there wanted to <u>stone</u> you; you are going back?" Jesus: "A day has twelve hours; those who walk in daylight do not stumble—they see by the daylight; if they walk during the night they stumble—they have no light
    C ¹¹⁻¹³ Lazarus has fallen asleep; I will go, wake him." disciples: "If he sleeps, Lord, he will get well" Jesus meant that Lazarus had died, they thought he meant natural sleep
      D ¹⁴⁻¹⁶ Jesus: "Lazarus is dead; for your sake I am glad that I was not with him, <u>so that you will believe</u>. Let us go to him." Thomas: "Let us all go and die with him"
        E ¹⁷ When Jesus arrived, Lazarus had been <u>buried four days</u>
          F ¹⁸⁻¹⁹ many Judeans had come to see Martha and Mary to comfort them
            G ²⁰⁻²¹ Martha heard that Jesus was coming, <u>went to meet him</u>
Martha: "<u>If you had been here, Lord, my brother would not have died</u>!
              H ²²⁻²⁴ <u>I know</u> that God will give you whatever you ask" Jesus: "Your brother will rise to life" she replied: "<u>I know</u> that he will rise to life on the last day"
                I ²⁵ Jesus: "I am the resurrection and the life
Those who <u>believe in me will live</u>, even though they <u>die</u>;
                  I ²⁶ those who <u>live and believe in me</u> will never <u>die</u>. Do you believe this?"
              H ²⁷ she answered "Yes, Lord! <u>I believe</u> that you are the Messiah, Son of God, who was to come into the world"
            G ²⁸⁻³² Martha called Mary. "The Teacher is asking for you." Mary <u>hurried out to meet him</u>; the people with Mary comforting her followed, thought she was going to the grave to weep. Mary fell at Jesus' feet: "<u>Lord, if you had been here, my brother would not have died</u>!"
          F ³³⁻³⁸ᵃ Jesus saw her, the people weeping; his heart was touched, troubled; Jesus: "Where have you buried him?" People: "Come and see, Lord." Jesus wept; people: "See how much he loved him!" some said, "He gave sight to the blind man; could he not have kept Lazarus from dying?" Deeply moved,
        E ³⁸ᵇ⁻³⁹ Jesus went to the tomb, a cave with a stone at the entrance: "Take the stone away!" Martha: "There will be a stench, Lord. He has been <u>buried four days</u>"
      D ⁴⁰⁻⁴² Jesus: "Didn't I tell you that you would see God's glory if you <u>believed</u>?" They took the stone away. Jesus: "I thank you, Father, that you hear me. I know that you always hear me, I say this for the sake of the people here, <u>so that they will believe</u> you sent me"
    C ⁴³⁻⁴⁵ After he said this, he called "Lazarus, come out!" He came out, his hands and feet wrapped in grave cloths, a cloth around his face; Jesus: "Untie him, let him go"
Many who came to visit Mary saw what Jesus did, believed in him
  B ⁴⁶⁻⁵³ Council: "What shall we do? If we let him go on, everyone will believe in him, Romans will destroy our Temple and nation!" Caiaphas, High Priest: "Fools! it is better that one man <u>die</u> for the people than for the nation to be destroyed"; prophesying that Jesus would <u>die</u> for the Jewish people, bring into one body all the scattered people of God
Jewish authorities made plans to <u>kill</u> Jesus
A ⁵⁴ Jesus did not travel openly in Judea, went to a town near the desert, Ephraim, where he stayed with the disciples

Figure 26. Raising of Lazarus (Sign 6)³

3. The story contains the fifth "I am" clause with predicates: "I am the resurrection and the life" (v. 25).

83

A Way of Reading John's Gospel

The center of the narrative contains Jesus' great resurrection claim, "I am the resurrection and the life." Martha did not have to wait for the last day: Jesus now, at this time, was the guarantor and definition of resurrection, and Martha's faith in him must yet undergo another quantum leap to manifest appropriate cognizance of this strikingly novel claim (v. 25, I; v. 26, I′). The central parallel statements indicate that mortal beings (biological creatures who die) and who believe in Jesus will receive a transformed immortal body, which is resurrection to eternal life.

Harris provides a paraphrase: Jesus said to her, that is, to Martha, "I myself am the pledge and the agent of resurrection; I myself am the giver of immortality to the resurrected dead. Accordingly, with regard to resurrection, the person who believes in me, even if death overtakes him, will nevertheless be raised up in resurrection life; and, with regard to immortality, every person who will gain resurrection life as a believer in me will never die and will live for ever."[4]

This story should explode all our earth-bound paradigms. Sickness, suffering, and death are intrinsic to this creation that necessarily fills our vistas. But this creation was going to be superseded. What Martha and Mary had learned was that the "future has burst into the present. The new creation, and with it the resurrection, has come forward from the end of time to the middle of time." Jesus had come not only from heaven to earth, but "from God's future into the present."[5]

---

4. Harris, *Raised*, 212.
5. Wright, *John, Part 2*, 7.

13

JOHN 12

Worship of Mary and Farewell to the Crowds

THE NEXT EPISODE IS a return to Bethany, back to the home of Lazarus and his sisters. We are told, significantly, that it was Passover time. The new Passover, and with it the new exodus, are imminent.

MARY'S AND JUDAS'S MOMENTS OF DECISION

The first incident related in this chapter (and the final three verses of the previous chapter) is composed of a chiastic structure featuring four separate players (fig. 27).

First, the hostile and scheming authorities set out to eliminate Jesus (11:56–57, A) and even to kill Lazarus (12:10–11, A'). Second, there is the new celebrity Lazarus, famously *raised from death*, eating with Jesus (12:1–2, B) and the object of curious fascination by many in the population (12:9, B'). Third, we read the vignette of Mary and her outrageously generous, worshipful, and prescient act of anointing Jesus with an expensive perfume, nard (12:3, C),[1] which elicited Jesus' unqualified approval (12:7–8, C').

---

1. According to Richard Chartres, nard was the main ingredient in the incense offered in Jewish temple worship; and so this event points to the true Temple, Jesus, who is now redolent with its fragrance (Chartres, referenced in

A Way of Reading John's Gospel

And finally, seemingly grossly out of place as the central element of the paragraph, is Judas the betrayer (12:4–5, D) and long-term thief (12:6, D′).

^{11:55} time for Passover Festival; many people went to Jerusalem to perform the ritual of purification

A ⁵⁶⁻⁵⁷ They were looking for Jesus; "He will not come to the festival?" <u>chief priests</u> and Phari<u>s</u>ees: if anyone knew where Jesus was, he should report it, so they could arrest him
  B ^{12:1-2} Six days before Passover, Jesus went to Bethany, home of <u>Lazarus</u>, whom <u>he had raised from death</u>; dinner there, <u>Lazarus</u> at table with Jesus
    C ³ <u>Mary</u> took a pint of expensive perfume, pure nard, poured it on Jesus' feet, wiped them with her hair; scent of perfume filled the house
      D ⁴⁻⁵ <u>Judas Iscariot</u>—going to betray him: "Why wasn't perfume sold for a year's wages, money given to <u>the poor</u>?"
      D′ ⁶ <u>He</u> did not say this because <u>he</u> cared about <u>the poor</u>; <u>he</u> was a thief, in charge of the common purse, helped <u>himself</u> from it
    C′ ⁷⁻⁸ Jesus said, "Leave <u>her</u> alone! <u>she</u> has saved this perfume for the day of my burial. You will always have poor people among you; will not always have me"
  B′ ⁹ people heard that Jesus was in Bethany, went there, because of Jesus, and to see <u>Lazarus, whom Jesus had raised from death</u>
A′ ¹⁰⁻¹¹ <u>chief priests</u> made plans to kill Lazarus, on his account many Jews were rejecting them, believing in Jesus.

Figure 27. Mary and Judas at the Hinge of History

If this is a valid chiastic structure, why should Judas occupy the center? Perhaps the author is making an appeal to his readers. The story of Jesus is nearing its climax. There is not much time left. Mary had a brief opportunity to show her devotion to Jesus, and she did this in an extravagant, unconventional way that always had the potential to expose her to criticism or ridicule. She grasped the moment—and could savor forever the joy of expressing her adoration of him. Judas also stood on the brink of the abyss. He had a window of opportunity in which he was free to choose between Jesus and money, but that would soon pass. The wrong decision would be catastrophic for him. Discussing this episode, Barclay said that there "is a time for doing and for saying things; and when that time is past, they can never be said and they can never be done."[2] Judas chose catastrophe.

Ford, *Gospel of John*, 233.

2. Barclay, *Gospel of John*, 2:131.

Mary and Judas provide a sharp contrast. She generously gave of her own resources; he selfishly grasped the resources of others. She saw (believed in) the worth of Jesus; he was blind to (disbelieved in) Jesus' surpassing worth. She was open, honest; he was conniving, duplicitous. She was motivated by love; he, by blind selfishness. She gained everything; he lost everything. Perhaps the author is saying to us, "Reader take note—everything depends on your current response to Jesus."

ENTRY OF THE KING AND HIS LAST APPEAL

In the second pericope, Jesus entered Jerusalem (vv. 12–19, fig. 28). He had previously absented himself when people's ill-considered revolutionary passions might have induced them to install Jesus as king (6:15). Now on his own terms, and in a context that he was controlling, he was acting to present himself as King but not the sort people had imagined. As we might expect in that emotional environment, the consequences of Jesus' action would be incendiary.

A 12 next day the large <u>crowd</u> that had come to the Passover Festival heard that Jesus was on his way to Jerusalem
   B 13 they took palm branches, went out to meet him shouting, "Praise God! God bless him who comes in the name of the Lord, the King of Israel!"
      C 14 Jesus found a donkey, rode on it, as <u>the scripture says</u>,
         D 15a "Do not be afraid, city of Zion!
         D' 15b your king is coming, riding a young donkey"
      C' 16 disciples did not understand this at the time; when Jesus was glorified, they remembered that <u>the scripture said</u> this about him, that they had done this for him
   B' 17 people with Jesus when he called Lazarus out of the grave, raised him from death, reported what had happened
A' 18-19 the <u>crowd</u> met him because they heard that he performed this sign. Pharisees: "We are not succeeding! Look, the world is running after him!"

Figure 28. Return of the King

This dramatic event develops (v. 12, A) and resolves (vv. 18–19, A') by describing the crowd that heard about Jesus. The

A Way of Reading John's Gospel

people broke out in adulation and excitement (v. 13, B; v. 17, B').[3] John provides the Scripture that provides an interpretation to what was going on (v. 14, C; v. 16, C'). This definitive Scripture is quoted at the center of the pericope: Jesus is bringing the opportunity of peace to the people of Jerusalem (v. 15a, D); as king, coming inoffensively on a donkey (v. 15b, D').[4]

The main pericope in chapter 12 describes Jesus' final public conversation with the crowds (fig. 29). As in 6:26-29 and 6:53-58, the first element introduces a concept that is greatly amplified and explored in the last. Here, some Greeks asked to *see* Jesus (vv. 20-21, A). Jesus' response initially seems somewhat tangential to the request. But in the discourse following, to *see* Jesus (to *believe* in him) is to recognize that his death is central to his own mission, and for the future of the whole world. And in the final element (vv. 35-42, A'), Jesus spoke about *light,* which is needed for seeing. Jesus urged his listeners to continue in the light (the truth that he embodied), to believe in it, and to be the people characterized by ordering their lives by it. The paragraph concludes with a warning from the prophet Isaiah about blindness (disbelief) and seeing (believing).[5] Isaiah himself was provided as the exemplar who answered the Greek's question: he *saw* the glory of Jesus.[6] The Greeks should look upon Jesus as Isaiah did. But Jesus' public engagement with the people ends on the haunting note of disbelief and rejection.

---

3. The waving of palm branches provides a provocative "political edge"; in 141 BC, branches and palm leaves festooned "Simon Maccabee's triumphal procession into the Jerusalem citadel" and expressed the people's joy at the rededication of the temple (1 Macc 13:51, 2 Macc 10:7). See Ford, *Gospel of John,* 236 and Wright, *John, Part 2,* 25.

4. See Zech 9:9; the passage also has echoes of Zeph 3:14-20.

5. Does God really blind people's eyes and close their minds (v. 40)? Ford sees this as hyperbolic language, a wake-up call to make people aware of their need before God. See Ford, *Gospel of John,* 247.

6. Isa 53:1, 6:10. In the Gospel of John, Isaiah is thus added to Abraham (8:56-58), Jacob (implied, 1:51; 4:12), Moses (1:45; 5:45-47), the prophets (1:45, 6:45), and of course John the Baptist (1: 8-9, 15, 29-30; 5:33) as seminally important figures of Israel's history who were said to witness to Jesus.

```
A 20-21 Greeks, at Jerusalem during the festival: "We want to see Jesus"
  B 22-23 Jesus to Philip, Andrew: "Hour has come for the Son of Man to receive glory
    C 24 truly: unless a grain of wheat is dropped in the ground and dies it remains alone;
    if it dies, it produces many grains
      D 25 Those who love their own life will lose it;
      those who hate their own life in this world will keep it for eternal life.
        E 26 Whoever serves me must follow me, that my servant will be with me where I am;
        my Father will honor anyone who serves me
          F 27 "My heart is troubled; shall I say, 'Father, save me from this hour'?
          F' But I came that I might go to this hour
        E' 28-30 Father, bring glory to your name!" voice from heaven, "I have brought
        glory to it, will do so again;" crowd heard the voice: thunder? an angel spoke?
        Jesus: "this voice spoke not for my sake but yours
      D' 31 Now is the time for this world to be judged;
      now the ruler of this world will be overthrown
    C' 32-33 When I am lifted up from the earth, I will draw everyone to me,"
    indicating kind of death by which he would die
  B' 34 crowd: "Messiah lives forever; how can the Son of Man be lifted up? who is Son of Man?"
A' 35-41 Jesus: "light among you a little longer; continue, believe in the light, be the people of the light;"
Jesus hid himself; had performed signs, they did not believe in him; Isaiah: "Lord, who believed our
message?" they were not able to believe; Isaiah: "God blinded their eyes, hardened their hearts; their eyes
would not see, their hearts would not understand, they would not turn to me to heal them;" Isaiah saw
Jesus' glory, his words referred to Jesus

42-43 many of the Jewish authorities believed Jesus; did not confess their faith, so as not to be expelled
from the synagogue; loved human approval, not God's
```

Figure 29. Last Appeal to the People

The second and second-to-last elements relate to the enigmatic figure of the Son of Man (v. 22, B; v. 34, B'). Jesus says that this person will receive glory—an anticipation of his own obedient death and resurrection. But the people cannot associate the victorious Messiah with anyone who will die, in particular by crucifixion, nor do they know the identity of this Son of Man.[7]

Jesus indicates that death is needed for life to ensue. The C elements focus on the necessity of death. Speaking metaphorically, a wheat seed must undergo involution—dissolution of its form, evacuation of its content—in the damp earth before the fruit-bearing plant appears from it (v. 24, C). Jesus identifies himself as that seed who will die and give life to many (vv. 32–33, C'). If the Greeks are to see Jesus, they must recognise that his terrible death is the way by which God will save the world.[8]

---

7. The son of man from Dan 7:13–14 was an apocalyptic figure uniting heaven and earth; the glory of Jesus as Son of Man would be seen in his incarnation, humiliating crucifixion, and resurrection. Ford, *Gospel of John*, 242.

8. Wright, *John, Part 2*, 29–30.

But the principle applies to the people in the crowd who listened to him. To give up one's life *in the world* is to gain it (v. 25, D). To hold to the status quo is death as *the world* imminently faces judgment (v. 31, D').

Finally, Jesus refers to and addresses the Father. Those who follow Jesus in his self-abnegation will be honored by the Father (v. 26, E). Jesus speaks of his anticipation that his servants will be with him where he is.[9] His followers also will be privileged to see the Father's glory (vv. 28–30, E').

The center of the pericope contains parallel statements (v. 27a, F). Jesus is troubled;[10] should he ask to be released from *this hour*?[11] The Father was the one to whom his thoughts were directed. No. The climax and meaning of his mission was to endure the sufferings of *this hour* (v. 27b, F'). And Jesus has now come to that climax.

Jesus' public activity finishes with a concluding summary (vv. 44–50, fig. 30). He has been doing the work of the one *who sent him*, and much depends on the people's acceptance of his message: they will enjoy the light, and be given eternal life. His Greek enquirers should know that to *see* (and hear) Jesus is to *see* (and hear) the Father himself (vv. 44–46, A; vv. 49–50, A').

Rejection of his message results in judgment (v. 47a, B; v. 48, B'). But Jesus has not come as judge but as Savior (v. 47b; C, C').[12] In this final appeal to believe, and his lament over those who did not believe, Jesus' time of engagement with the populace of Israel has come to its close.

---

9. This is the first of three times in John's Gospel when Jesus expresses the desire that his disciples would be with him. See also 14:3; 17:24.

10. The very state of mind he urged his disciples to resist; 14:1, 27.

11. The same distress expressed in Jesus' prayer in Gethsemane; Mark 14:32–42 and parallels in Matt and Luke.

12. Cf. 3:17.

A ⁴⁴⁻⁴⁶ Jesus: "Whoever believes in me believes in <u>him who sent me</u>; Whoever sees me sees <u>him who sent me</u>. I have come into the world as light; no one who believes in me should remain in the dark
    B ⁴⁷ If people hear <u>my words</u>, but <u>do not obey</u> them, I will not <u>judge</u> them
        C I did not come to judge the world
        C' but [I came] to save it
    B' ⁴⁸ Those who reject me, do <u>not accept</u> <u>my words</u>, have one who will <u>judge</u> them; the word I have spoken will be their <u>judge</u> on the last day
A' ⁴⁹⁻⁵⁰ I have not spoken on my own authority; the <u>Father who sent me</u> commanded me what to say; his command leads to eternal life. What I say is what the Father has told me to say"

Figure 30. Concluding Summary of Jesus' Mission

14

JOHN 13–17

Farewell to the Disciples

JOHN'S GOSPEL MOVES TO Jesus' extended conversation alone with his disciples. Brouwer has stated that Jesus' teaching in the upper room is presented chiastically. In outline, "the repetitive and reflexive elements of the Johannine farewell discourse fit together in a large chiasm bounded by expressions of spiritual intimacy with God on either end (the foot-washing episode of chapter 13 and the prayer of chapter 17) and channeled toward the challenge to 'abide' in Jesus at the center (15:1–17)."[1]

Starting from this general pattern, the finer outline of the Farewell Discourse (as I see it) is depicted in the outline scheme and in table 4 below. There are seven parts to this conversation. Each subsection seems to possess *one* key phrase that indicates its purpose. This phrase is words of Jesus: "I have *told* you this *so that* . . ." The one exception is the first subsection that describes Jesus' foot-washing *action* (13:1–17). Jesus has taught essential theology by *enacting* the paradigm of humble service, and following the performance of this practical deed, he said, "I have *set an example* for you *so that* you will do . . ." (v. 15).

---

1. Brouwer, "Understanding Chiasm," 99–100.

JOHN 13-17

1 Jesus serves
  2 Betrayal to glory
    3 Love of God
      4 Unity with Jesus the vine
    5 Hatred of the world
  6 Sadness to gladness
7 Jesus Prays

Table 4. A Possible Chiastic Structure of the Farewell Discourse

Section	Possible title	Key verse (GNT, italics added)	Ref.
13:1–17	Jesus serves	"I have set an example for you, *so that* you will do just what I have done for you."	13:15
13:18–32	Betrayal to glory	"I tell you this now before it happens, *so that* you will believe that 'I Am Who I Am.'"	13:19
13:33—14:31	Love of the triune God	"I have told you this now before it all happens, *so that* when it does happen, you will believe."	14:29
15:1–17	Unity with the vine	"I have told you this *so that* my joy may be in you and that your joy may be complete."	15:11
15:18—16:4a	Hatred of the world	"I have told you this *so that* you will not give up your faith" / "you will remember."	16:1, 4a
16:4b–33	Sadness to gladness	"I have told you this, *so that* you will have peace by being united to me."	16:33
17:1–26	Jesus prays	"I say these things in the world *so that* they may have my joy in their hearts."	17:13

1. JESUS SERVES, 13:1–17

Carson emphasizes the uneasiness and tension that must have prevailed at the Last Supper.[2] The necessary formality of washing the guests' feet was strictly a servant's job. That Jesus, the master, should have been the one to perform this servile role was acutely embarrassing to the disciples.

Following a solemn description of the setting—it was Passover time (the celebration of the exodus, Israel's formative

2. Carson, *Jesus*, 11–16.

event)—we are told that Jesus' long-awaited hour had arrived. That is, Jesus was going to the Father, and he was going to show how he loved his disciples to the end (that is, both "utterly" and "to the point of death").[3]

The story of Jesus' foot-washing action is described in chiastic form (fig. 31). The first (v. 3, A) and concluding (vv. 13–14, A') elements are about the supremacy of Jesus. There is the paradox that Jesus knew he had complete power. Despite the fearsome darkness coming over him, he could see through it to a victory on the other side. Two themes of the Gospel are juxtaposed here: Jesus knew he had *come from* the Father (in incarnation) and was *going to* the Father (in death and resurrection). The account concludes with the challenge of Jesus as teacher and Lord, albeit (so counter-intuitively!) of a servant variety.

1-2 Setting: Day before Passover, the hour to leave this world, go to the Father

A ³ Jesus' complete power: from/going to God
  B ⁴⁻⁶ rose from table, took off outer garment
    C ⁷ Jesus' assurance: you will understand later
      D ⁸ᵃ Peter's confusion: don't wash
        E ⁸ᵇ Jesus: be washed to be my disciple
      D' ⁹ Peter's confusion: wash head and hands
    C' ¹⁰⁻¹¹ Jesus' assurance: you are clean
  B' ¹² outer garment on, return to table
A' ¹³⁻¹⁷ Jesus, teacher and Lord: washed feet; you should wash one another's feet; I have set an example so that [*hina*] you will do what I have done for you—you are happy if you do them

Figure 31. Jesus Serves

The layers of the story proceed through Jesus' dramatic interchange with his disciples. Jesus left (vv. 4–6, B) and returned to (v. 12, B') the dinner table. He provided comforting assurance that the disciples would come to understand what his servanthood meant

3. Ford, *Gospel of John*, 254.

(v. 7, C), and that it entailed his making them clean (vv. 10–11, C′). This theological meaning of "washing" was held in relief by Peter's incapacity to go beyond the physical meaning of being washed (v. 8a, D; v. 9, D′).

The center of the chiasm (v. 8b, E) states the truth that Jesus must cleanse these men—remove their sin, their impurity before God—before they can be his disciples. We may note that "the water of the foot-washing, like the water of the wedding at Cana in Galilee, has been made the symbol of the purification wrought by the sacrificial death of Jesus, and by that alone."[4]

The "so that" (Greek, *hina*) statement concludes the paragraph with the practical imperative arising from Jesus' action. The humble servanthood shown by Jesus is the paradigm by which his followers must live. In the church of Jesus, true authority is revealed in self-denying humble service. If we want to be church leaders, in the first instance we don't go to a seminar or a seminary. We identify people who are in need and care for them. Those who serve as Jesus has served are happy, fortunate, blessed (v. 17). This is one of only two beatitudes in John's Gospel.[5]

2. BETRAYAL TO GLORY, 13:18–32

The second act of the scene follows immediately. Jesus introduces the fearsome prospect that he will be betrayed by one of his disciples (v. 18) and immediately follows that up with the second *hina* statement. He must emphasise without delay that the perfidy is not a meaningless act of treachery, but it is in fact written into the vocation to which he has been called, and it will serve an overarching purpose. "I tell you this now before it happens, *so that* when it does happen, you will believe that I Am Who I Am" (v. 19). This is the sixth absolute "I am" statement in the Gospel. Jesus' anticipation of the terrible event will confirm that he acts knowingly, as divinity, in full awareness of what is approaching.

---

4. Marsh, *Saint John*, 485.
5. The other being 20:29; Ford, *Gospel of John*, 412.

A Way of Reading John's Gospel

The story proceeds in nested and inverted form (fig. 32). This strange paragraph starts and finishes with Jesus' identifying himself with his Father. To receive Jesus is to receive his Father (v. 20, A; cf. 1:12). To reveal Jesus' glory is to reveal the glory of his Father (vv. 31–32, A'; cf. 1:14).

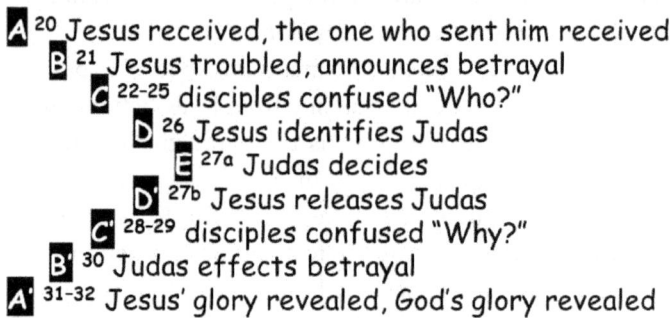

18-19 Setting, betrayal: I tell you this now, so that [*hina*] you will believe that "I Am Who I Am"

A **20** Jesus received, the one who sent him received
  B **21** Jesus troubled, announces betrayal
    C **22-25** disciples confused "Who?"
      D **26** Jesus identifies Judas
        E **27a** Judas decides
      D' **27b** Jesus releases Judas
    C' **28-29** disciples confused "Why?"
  B' **30** Judas effects betrayal
A' **31-32** Jesus' glory revealed, God's glory revealed

Figure 32. Betrayal to Glory[6]

The plot develops. The next elements describe the approaching crisis of treachery. First, the betrayal is announced by Jesus, who was said to be deeply troubled (v. 21, B). Second, the betrayal is effected by Judas (v. 30, B'). At this solemn moment (as Wright notes), the powers of darkness entered Judas and he went out into the night.[7] "The door opens on to the dark night, in every sense and at every level, and Judas disappears into it."[8] The other disciples were confused as to what was happening. They asked "Who?" (vv. 22–25, C) and "Why?" (vv. 28–29, C') as Jesus addressed Judas—identifying him (v. 26, D) and commissioning him (v. 27b, D') as the betrayer.

---

6. Verse 19 contains the sixth absolute "I am" statement. The GNT expresses this as "I Am Who I Am"; other versions (JB, NIV, RSV) as "I am He." Either way, a claim to divinity is indicated.

7. Wright, *John, Part 2*, 39.

8. Wright, *John, Part 2*, 52.

The crux of this section is Judas's decision to carry out his treacherous plan. Why should that depraved decision be the crux of the story (v. 27a, E)? Perhaps it is just the central feature of the drama. Or perhaps it demonstrates the paradox that even Judas's freely chosen evil action is going to be used by God for his redemptive and life-giving purposes. The depths of evil are not beyond God's capacity to create newness and beauty. The betrayal of Jesus was somehow written into the history of the universe. God brings new things out of the disastrously misused freedom of his creatures.

3. LOVE OF GOD, 13:33—14:31

The first major block of Jesus' teaching was to prepare his disciples for the painful time of separation that was imminent. It is based on the tiny word *go*, by which Jesus indicated his *going*, his return to the Father by way of his sacrificial death and resurrection. As Carson says, "Jesus' departure from them [his going] is his return to the glory rightly his, by way of the cross and the tomb."[9]

The structure of this section is complex (fig. 33). It starts and finishes in chiastic mode, but the central section is based on several mini-chiasms which are centered around three questions from the disciples. The questions of Thomas, Philip, and Judas (not Iscariot) seem to be redundant, because Jesus has, in each case, just provided the answer to their question. The disciples' questions thus provide the occasion for Jesus to reiterate, and to elaborate on, his earlier statements. The chiastic structure (teaching, question, repeated teaching) may be useful (perhaps) to help us, non-insightful readers, to latch on to Jesus' all-important message.

---

9. Carson, *Jesus*, 19; see also Wright, *John, Part 2*, 63.

A Way of Reading John's Gospel

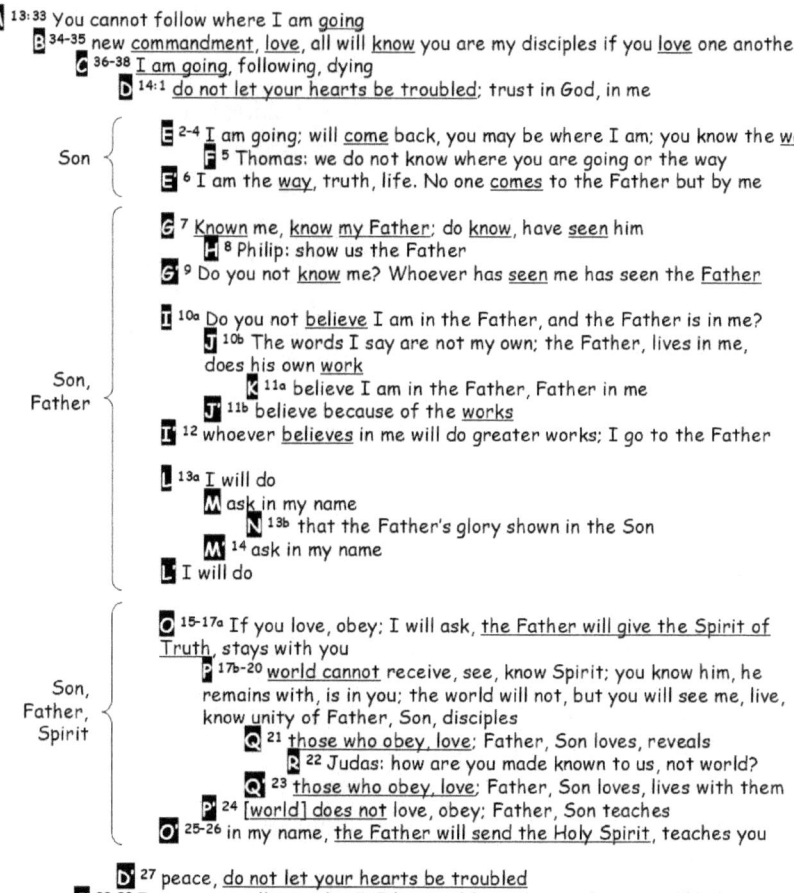

Figure 33. The Love of the Triune God[10]

10. Love is featured in the paired elements of vv. 13:34–35 and 14:31a (B, B'), of v. 21 and v. 23 (Q, Q'), and in the summary verse 14:15. This section contains the sixth "I am" saying, with predicates; namely "the way, the truth and the life" (14:6). The Greek word *paracletos*, referring to the Holy Spirit (v. 15, O; v. 26, O'), is translated *helper* (GNT), *advocate* (JB), one who *stands by you* (JBP), and *counselor* (NIV, RSV).

The first (13:33, A) and last (14:31b, A') elements are about *going*. In the first, Jesus indicated that the disciples could not follow him. Jesus was going to death, a vocation written into the history of the universe, to be fulfilled by him alone. Jesus was uniquely bearing the evil and brokenness of the world. In any case, the disciples were not prepared for the ordeal that was coming, and they would fail to go with him, and scatter. But at the end of the section, Jesus invited the disciples to accompany him: "Let us go."[11] When they had taken the intervening teaching to heart and had made sense of it in the light of his resurrection, they would truly go with him in his salvific mission and ultimately arrive at the Father's place, perhaps via their own life-sacrifice.[12]

The second (13:34-35, B) and penultimate (14:30-31a, B') elements develop the theme of God's commandment to love. In the first case, it is a *new* commandment because it is to be modelled on the love of Jesus himself.[13] It is an imperative given to the disciples, so the world will *know* of their devotion to Jesus. In the second case, it is exemplified by Jesus himself, so that the world will *know* of his obedience to the Father. Love is the inner dynamic of mission, but regularly ignored by Jesus' wayward followers.

The next pair of elements returns to the theme of Jesus' *going*, and repeats the ideas of the first (A) and last (A') elements. In 13:36-38 (C), the disciples' incomprehension about this *going* was exemplified by Peter, who protested that he would follow Jesus anywhere.[14] Jesus indicated that Peter could not follow him

---

11. Scholars have offered many (seemingly forced) explanations for Jesus' statement in v. 31b. See Carson, *Jesus*, 85-87. But when this section is read chiastically, the call "Let us go" anticipates the time when the sad acknowledgment "You cannot go" (13:33) will be past, and Jesus' true disciples will indeed walk the path of suffering obedience in Jesus' footsteps, going to sacrificial service and ultimately to God's home.

12. In the Synoptic Gospels, Jesus also seems to point to the initial inability of the disciples to follow him, and the subsequent reality of their doing so (Mark 10:38-39, Matt 20:22-23).

13. Wright, *John, Part 2*, 55; see also 1 John 2:7-8; 3:11, 16-17; 4:7-10.

14. Verney, *Water into Wine*, 156; Peter said he would lay down his life for Jesus (13:37)—just as Jesus said he would lay down his life for the sheep (10:11, 15). Peter represents us all in our pathetic self-confidence.

at that time (and would in fact dissociate himself from Jesus) but would follow him later. In 14:28-29 (C'), Jesus reiterated that he was returning to the Father (in death and resurrection), and he followed this up by the key "so that" statement: "I have told you this now before it all happens, *so that* when it does happen, you will believe" (v. 29). Jesus' death was not to be seen as a cause of despair but as the basis of faith, of trusting confidence, in God's saving activity.

The fourth pair of elements (14:1, D; v. 27, D') comprise a direct parallelism. They have in common the injunction that the disciples should not be worried and upset. On three previous occasions, Jesus has been said to be troubled (11:33, 12:27, 13:21). Is Jesus handing out cheap advice, mere platitudes that he himself could not practice? No. Jesus was entering the deepest darkness, the utmost horror of bearing the world's sin and, concomitantly, separation from his Father.[15] These were agonies the disciples could never know. The disciples' part was to believe, to trust. Jesus' part was to make the sacrifice that would give them his serene peace, the confidence that he had won the ultimate victory over evil.

Having negotiated these four paired outer elements, we reach the central part of the chapter. This is divided into three subsections. The first, with a question from Thomas, is about the Son. The second, with a request from Philip, is about the relationship of Son and Father. The third, with a question from Judas (not Iscariot), is about the Son, Father, and Spirit. It is undeniably trinitarian. Do not let anyone try to argue that the idea of the triune God is a late (post-biblical) innovation!

First, Jesus described the spaciousness of the Father's house[16] (explicitly, the destination to which Jesus was going), and how he would conduct his disciples there. Jesus' role was to be the way or means to get to that destination, so that they would be with him where he would be (14:2-4, E). Thomas was floundering in his

---

15. This understanding was triggered by Verney, *Water into Wine*, 150.

16. It is suggested that the believer's dwelling place (Greek, *monē*; used only in 14:2 and 14:23 in the entire New Testament) is located in the love of Jesus himself (Ford, *Gospel of John*, 272).

understanding, but he saw just enough light to ask where Jesus was going and how the disciples could follow him there (v. 5, F). Jesus' answer repeated his earlier statement but made it more explicit. Jesus was that way (and also the truth that revealed that way and the life that enabled people to traverse it). This is the sixth of the "I am" sayings with predicates. And the destination was the Father (v. 6, E'). Thank you, Thomas; Jesus has made himself very clear.

Second, Jesus stated that to know (or see) him was to know (or see) the Father (v. 7, G). Philip could not process this astonishing equation. His interest was excited by the idea of seeing the Father, but he could not assimilate the notion that this God was manifested and known in his familiar teacher (v. 8, H). In response to Philip's incomprehension, Jesus again repeated his claim in unambiguous terms. Anyone who knows Jesus in fact knows the Father in all his divine mystery (v. 9, G').

The closeness of Jesus and the Father is elaborated in two following mini-chiasms (vv. 10–12 and vv. 13–14). In the first, the emphasis is on *believing* that the Son and the Father live in the closest intimacy (are *in* each other, v. 10a, I; Jesus is going *to* the Father, v. 12, I'), and this closeness of relationship is reiterated in the central element (v. 11a, K). This intimacy should be recognized because the Son's actions (which include his speech) are the very actions of his Father (v. 10b, J; v. 11b J').[17]

And, finally, the actions of Jesus (what he will *do*), in response to the disciples' fervent dedication to him, will reveal the glory that is shared by the Son and the Father (vv. 13–14). When Jesus says, "I will do whatever you ask for," he is not offering a blank check. Rather, prayers "in his name" are prayers inspired by the nature of Jesus.[18] They are prayers that arise from knowing Jesus, and from

---

17. But how can we do greater works than Jesus? From the example he provided by washing the disciples' feet, his followers can exceed it quantitatively (around the world, through history) and qualitatively (by growth in "humility, in loving service" by intimacy with Jesus and his loving Father—"because I am going to the Father"). Ford, *Gospel of John*, 281.

18. Ford, *Gospel of John*, 281.

"being drawn into his life and love and sense of purpose" and that are concerned only with his and his Father's glory.[19]

Third, a thoroughly trinitarian exchange completes the section, leading to the central focus (Judas's question, vv. 22, R). Jesus teaches that anyone who truly loves Jesus will obey him; to such obedient people, Jesus will ask the Father to send the Holy Spirit who reveals the truth (vv. 15–17a, O);[20] but the disobedient world will be completely oblivious of the Spirit's presence and illumination (vv. 17b–20, P). Jesus then reinforces what he has said in v. 15: it is only those who love and obey who live in loving, illuminating fellowship with the Father and the Son (v. 21, Q). At this point Judas, sensing what is going on, but not seeing it clearly, asks the question for which Jesus has just provided the answer (v. 22, R).

And in the second part of the chiasm, Jesus' answer to Judas provides the same teaching, although in reverse order. Let's make this very clear. First, to love Jesus is to obey him. The result of obedience is intimacy with the Son and the Father (v. 23, Q'). Second, to fail to love and obey—the characteristic of the unbelieving world—is a rejection of the illuminating revelation that comes from the Son and the Father (v. 24, P'). Third, it is the Holy Spirit sent in the name of the Son (that is, on the Son's authority) by the Father who instructs the obedient disciple (v. 26, O').

So how does Jesus reveal himself to his followers and not to the world (Judas's question)? The loving obedience of the true disciple leads to intimacy with God, and the Holy Spirit comes to lead those disciples into God's liberating truth. There seems to be a positive feed-forward loop: obedience to intimacy to the revealing Spirit to new vistas of obedience ...

---

19. Wright, *John, Part 2*, 64.

20. Jesus calls the Spirit the Helper (GNT; Greek, *parakletos*). This term has two meanings. It could be translated "encourager," but also "may well have legal connotations and suggest a legal 'advocate' who stands with his client when under trial." Wenham and Walton, *Exploring*, 268. The Advocate "stands beside us and speaks on our behalf before our accusers." Verney, *Water into Wine*, 160.

4. UNITY WITH JESUS THE VINE, 15:1-17

The central part of the discourse is the extended metaphor[21] of the grapevine. It seems to be a development of the themes arising from the previous subsection: love and obedience, closeness with Jesus, and the outcome of such union in the lives of disciples (in this case, fruitfulness). The dominant theme is that the disciples *remain in union with* (that is, *abide in*, live in the closet intimacy with) Jesus.[22]

An opening statement introduces the theme. The metaphor of the vine was used frequently in the Hebrew Scriptures. The vine was Israel, called, commissioned, and blessed by God—but regularly chided for its failures and its unfruitfulness and subject to divine judgment. In contrast, Jesus presented himself as the true vine, the representative of Israel, the fulfilment of everything good that Israel was intended (but failed) to be and to manifest.[23] Jesus was "the one on whom God's purposes are now resting . . . Israel-in-person."[24]

The sermon about the vine seems to comprise two parts, each tending to show chiastic symmetry (fig. 34). In the first part, Jesus described branches that are fruitless (and are removed) and others that are fruitful and are pruned so as to increase their productivity (v. 2, A; v. 6, A'). The secret to fruitfulness is to remain in the closest unity with Jesus (vv. 3-4, B; v. 5b, B'). The key to this metaphor is that Jesus is the vine, and the ever-dependent branches are his faithful disciples (v. 5a, C). But what is this *fruit* that disciples are supposed to bear? To Marsh, it is every manifestation of the Messiah-centered life: to bear fruit is "to be with the Lord in witness, both in word and in deed, in action and in passion, in suffering and in joy, in defeat and victory, in death and resurrection."[25] The fruit is a life lived in joyful and unrestrained obedience to God.

21. It is not a parable, as is often indicated; see Carson, *Jesus*, 89.

22. The verb *menein* (remain) is used eleven times in this section of text; see Ford, *Gospel of John*, 293.

23. Ps 80:8-16; Hos 10:1; Isa 5:1-7; Jer 2:21; 12:10-13; Ezek 15; 19:10-14; Carson, *Jesus*, 89-90.

24. Wright, *John, Part 2*, 70.

25. Marsh, *Saint John*, 520.

¹ Setting: Jesus the vine; Father the gardener

A ² fruitless and fruitful branches
  B ³⁻⁴ "You are clean, remain in me [Jesus] to bear fruit
    C ⁵ᵃ I am the vine, you are the branches
  B' ⁵ᵇ remain in me to bear fruit
A' ⁶ fruitless and fruitful branches

D ⁷ ask and receive
  E ⁸ bear fruit to be my disciples
    F ⁹ love defined: I love you as the Father loves me
      G ¹⁰ obey commands, remain in love
        H ¹¹ have told you this so that [hina] joy complete
      G' ¹² my command: love one another
    F' ¹³ love defined: to lay down your life
  E' ¹⁴⁻¹⁶ᵃ obey commands (bear fruit) to be my friends
D' ¹⁶ᵇ ask and receive"

¹⁷ my command: love one another

Figure 34. Unity with Jesus the Vine[26]

The second chiasm commences (v. 7, D) and concludes (v. 16b, D') with the assurance that whatever the disciples ask of the Father in Jesus' name will be given to them.[27] Again, it must be acknowledged that God is not beholden to our typically ignorant and selfish barrage of requests (our incessant asking). The inappropriateness of our asking suggests that we should interpret Jesus' assurance to mean that when we live in union with Jesus, our asking becomes conformed to the values of God, to the mores of heaven.[28] Continual pruning or discipline leads us to ask for only those

---

26 This central component of Jesus' discourse includes the seventh and final "I am" saying with a predicate: the vine.

27. Jesus' "ask and you shall receive" theme is evidenced abundantly also in the Synoptic Gospels; see Mark 11:24; Matt 7:7–8; and Luke 11:9–10.

28. We should ask in Jesus' name, as his representatives who desire what he desires. "If we dwell in his love, and if his commandments are dwelling in us, then we should ask for what it is we desire . . . because what you desire is what

things that are divine priorities, God's own commitments, such as the revelation of his glory, the establishment of God's own rule of love, justice, and peace, and the disciples' growth in holiness. If remaining in union with Jesus is needed to bear fruit (v. 4, B; v. 5, B'), and also the precondition for receiving whatever we ask for in prayer (v. 7, D; v. 16b, D') then perhaps our prayers should be directed to the bearing of fruit (preeminently sacrificial love) in our lives.

Jesus' teaching about the bearing of fruit and obedience to his commandments transforms his listeners into being his real disciples (v. 8, E) and indeed, astonishingly, into being his friends (vv. 14–16a, E'). Jesus defines true love. It is the relationship he has with the Father and that he has with his disciples (v. 9, F). And in terms of action, love is to be seen in the imminent giving of his life in sacrifice for his disciples (v. 13, F'). Such unreserved love is the paradigm that Jesus disciples' are to follow. Obedience to Jesus' commandments and the expression of love are inseparable (v. 10, G; v. 12, G').

The central element of the central subsection of the discourse is the "so that" (*hina*) statement. The disciples' joy should be complete when they live in union with Jesus (v. 11, H).[29] The prospect of joy seems incongruously pregnant with sweet anticipation as the disciples must work in a threatening and hostile environment.

5. HATRED OF THE WORLD, 15:18—16:4A

We come to a strange paradox. Jesus' people have been enjoined to cultivate and live in love. But they will be hated by the unbelieving world. We can understand this animosity when Jesus' followers engage in love talk that is hypocritical. But Jesus indicates in the fifth section of the discourse that such hatred is to be expected— because Jesus himself is hated. A pattern of this unidirectional

---

the Father himself desires, and as you commit your energy to make it happen your will is aligned with his will." Verney, *Water into Wine*, 159; cf. 163.

29. A wonderful truth learned well by John and expressed also in 1 John 1:4.

A Way of Reading John's Gospel

hatred is demonstrated already in the New Testament. Evans indicates that the earliest history of the church may be interpreted as the ongoing opposition of the powerful family of the high priest Annas to the family and community of Jesus.[30]

This somber section starts with a mini-chiasm (fig. 35). The disciples were being prepared for the world's hatred (v. 18a, A; v. 19e, A'). The reason for this animosity is that Jesus himself is the primary object of their hatred (v. 18b, B), which is directed also to those who are identifiable as his followers (v. 19d, B'). As a result of Jesus' call, the community of Jesus does not *belong* to the world (v. 19a, C; v. 19c, C'). If Jesus' disciples belonged to the world, they would be loved by it (v. 19b, D), but the world recognizes them as aliens. This is a no-compromise situation.

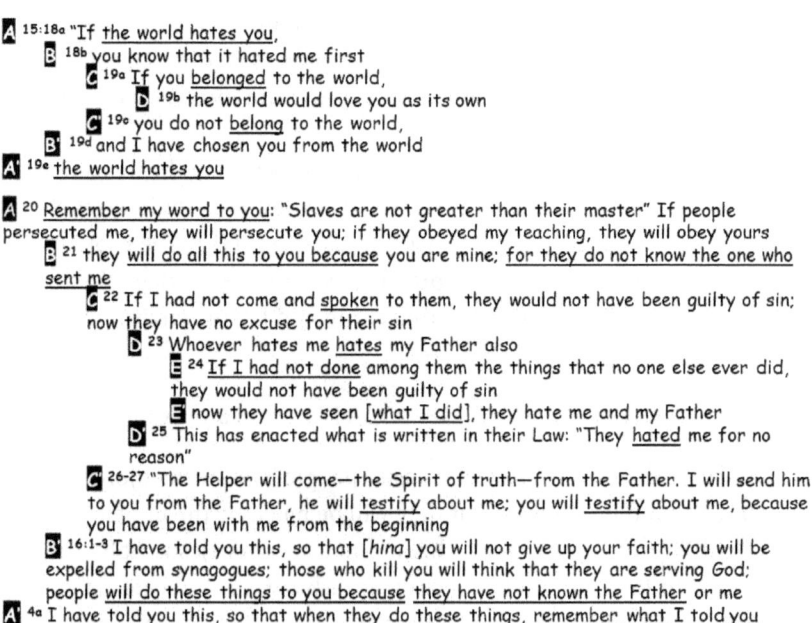

Figure 35. Hatred of the World

---

30. Evans, *Jesus to the Church*, 1-2, 13-16, 94-115.

The main body of teaching both starts (15:20, A) and concludes (16:4a, A′) with Jesus' appeal to the disciples' memories. "Remember what I told you." Even after he has been taken from them, they are to be cognizant of his warning. Persecution must not take them by surprise. There is no "health and wealth" gospel here; it looks as if authentic discipleship will be characterized by an abundance of strain and pain.

The next pair of elements (15:21, B; 16:1–3, B′) harks back to Judas' question in 14:22, when he asked how Jesus would reveal himself to the disciples but not to the world. Jesus stated that the world will do its worst because *they do not know the Father or Jesus himself*. The key *hina* statement is given in 16:1. Jesus has spoken of the impeding hatred and suffering *so that* his disciples would not abandon their faith in him. Expect the world's animosity. Practice endurance. Be faithful—even though, for Western Christians, conflict with the world usually comes as seduction to compromise, not overt belligerence.[31]

The world is culpable, guilty of sin, because Jesus has *spoken* to them (15:22, C). The Spirit sent by the Father will continue to *speak* (witness) to them, as indeed the disciples will share in this ongoing witness to the world (v. 26–27, C′).

Jesus reiterated the fact of the world's *hatred* toward both him and his Father (v. 23, D; v. 25, D′). In the latter verse, Jesus quotes "their Law."[32] This indicates that *the world* in this context refers to the Jewish authorities. Gentile hatred will come in due course. He then repeats the charge of world's culpability in near-parallel central elements of the paragraph. The people of the world are guilty because their animus remains implacable despite the things Jesus has *done* among them (24a, E) and which they themselves witnessed (24b, E′).

---

31. Perhaps the *hina* statement (16:1) pertains to the promise of the Holy Spirit (15:26–27). Confidence that the Spirit has come to speak of Jesus ensures enduring stability for the faith of Jesus' disciples.

32. This is probably the Septuagint translation of Ps 69:4 or 35:19; see Ford, *Gospel of John*, 303.

6. SADNESS TO GLADNESS, 16:4B–33

Jesus' final words to his disciples seem to be arranged in a complex chiasm (A-B-C-D-D'-C'-B'-A') (fig. 36). The structure of this section of the discourse seems to be based on Jesus' solemn four-fold indication of what he has (or has not) *told* his followers (vv. 4b, 12, 25, 33). In three instances, Jesus' teaching points are highlighted by his disciples' inability to comprehend what he says (vv. 5b–6 in B; vv. 17–19, between D and D'; and vv. 29–30 in B'). The disciples' lack of understanding is, each time, portrayed at the center of a small chiastic subunit that comprises the elements B and B', and that includes D and D'. Jesus makes a statement, the disciples evince a lack of understanding, and Jesus elaborates on the initial idea. We have seen already how the disciples' dullness acts as a foil to highlight key aspects of Jesus' teaching.[33]

We will work through this chapter in a way that differs from that of other chiasms. Jesus' four statements referring to what he has (or, *has not*) told them follow below in (linear) order. An initial summary of the chapter is shown for clarification.

> 4b "I did not *tell* you these things"
>> 5b–6 Disciples silent, sad
>
> 12 "I have more to *tell* you"
>> 17–19 Disciples: "What does this 'little while' mean?"
>
> 25 "I have used figures of speech to *tell* you these things"
>> 29–30 Disciples: "This makes us believe that you came from God"
>
> 33 "I have *told* you this so that you will have peace"

First, Jesus said: "I did not tell you these things, for I was with you" (v. 4b, A). The time of separation had arrived, and certain things needed to be said.

---

33. As we have observed in John 13:33—14:31.

John 13-17

A ⁴ᵇ "<u>I did not tell you these things</u> at first, for I was with you
  B ⁵ᵃ But now <u>I am going</u> to him who sent me
    ⁵ᵇ⁻⁶ *none of you asks me where <u>I am going</u>; I have told you, you are full of grief*
  ⁷⁻¹¹ Truly: it is better for you that <u>I go</u>; <u>if I do not go</u>, the Helper will not come; <u>if I go</u>, I will send him to you; when he comes, he will show the world it is wrong about sin (they do not believe in me), what is right (<u>I am going</u> to the Father, you will see me no more), judgment (the ruler of this world has been judged)

   C ¹²⁻¹⁵ "<u>I have more to tell you</u>—too much to bear. When the Spirit of truth <u>comes</u>, he will lead you into all truth; will not speak on his own authority; will speak of what he hears, tell you of things to come, give me glory, take what I say and tell it to you. All that my Father has is mine; that is why I said the Spirit will take what is mine and tell it to you
      D ¹⁶ "In a little while you will <u>see</u> me no more; a little while later you will <u>see</u> me"
         ¹⁷⁻¹⁹ *disciples: "What does this mean—'in a little while you will not <u>see</u> me, a little while later you will <u>see</u> me, I am going to the Father'?"*
      D' ²⁰⁻²⁴ "Truly: you will weep, the world will be glad; your sadness will turn to gladness; a woman giving birth is sad, when the baby is born, she is happy; now you are sad, I will <u>see</u> you again, your hearts will be filled with gladness. In that day, truly: the Father will give you what you ask in my name: ask, you will receive, your happiness complete

   C' ²⁵⁻²⁷ "<u>I have used metaphors to tell you these things</u>; the time <u>will come</u> when I will not use metaphors but will speak plainly about the Father; When that day <u>comes</u>, you will ask him in my name; the Father loves you because you love me, have believed that I came from God
  B' ²⁸ I <u>came</u> from the Father, <u>came</u> into the world; now I am leaving the world, <u>going</u> to the Father."
    ²⁹⁻³⁰ *disciples: "Now you are speaking plainly, without metaphors. We know now that you know everything, questions not needed; we believe that you <u>came from</u> God"*
  ³¹⁻³² Jesus: "Do you believe? The time is coming, is already here, when you will be scattered; I will be alone—but the Father is with me

A' ³³ <u>I have told you this</u> so that [*hina*] you will have peace in union with me. The world will make you suffer. Be brave! I have defeated the world!"

Figure 36. Sadness to Gladness³⁴

34 The mini-chiasms (within B and B' and between D and D'), are structured around the disciples' reactions, shown by indents and italics. An analysis of this chiasm typical of those discussed elsewhere is as follows: In the first and last elements, Jesus speaks of what he had not until now told the disciples (v. 4b, A) and why he has now told it—that his disciples would have his peace, the sixth *hina* statement (v. 33, A'). In the second (vv. 5-11, B) and second-to-last (vv. 28-32, B') elements, Jesus speaks of his imminent going and where he has come from. In the third (vv. 12-15, C) and third-to-last (vv. 25-27, C') elements, Jesus speaks of what he has told in part but looks to the future when the Spirit comes and when intimacy with the Father will provide full illumination. The central elements (vv. 16-24, D and D') address *not seeing* (sadness) and *seeing* (gladness that cannot be taken away).

A Way of Reading John's Gospel

A discussion followed on Jesus' *going* away from the disciples (vv. 5a–11, B). Jesus stated that his *going* was imminent ("now," v. 5a). The disciples seemed to take this *going* without comment, but were evidently downcast (vv. 5b–6). Jesus then repeated that he is *going*, but he assured them that this was a good thing because the Holy Spirit would come to them (vv. 7–11). The Spirit would show the people of the world that they are wrong about sin (the human condition that necessitated the death of Jesus and that reached its greatest extent when people failed to believe in Jesus), righteousness (Jesus has overcome sin and his victory has been demonstrated) and judgment (in Jesus' death, it is the powers of evil that have been judged and destroyed).[35]

Wright has contextualized the Spirit's work through the church in the present day: "How do we shape a generation through which the spirit will convict the world of sin (in the face of Western arrogance and assumed moral superiority), of justice (in a world where biblical meaning, justice for the poor, has been obliterated by justice in the shape of state-sanctioned violence), and of judgment (in a culture that acts as if it were the arbiter of truth)?"[36] The suffering, death, and resurrection of Jesus must be paradigmatic of the way we live today.[37]

Jesus subsequently stated that he had "more to tell" the disciples, although at that time they still would be unable to face those truths (vv. 12–15, C). He reiterated that the Spirit would come (vv. 13–15) in order to lead believers into all truth—God's truth understood in its widest sense—and to make known the glory of Jesus. The truth that they could not absorb now would be taught by the Spirit in the future.

---

35. Marsh, *Saint John*, 535–37, 540. Expressed another way, to reject Jesus is the root of sin; the relationship of Jesus with his Father reveals the nature of righteousness; in the judgment passed on Jesus the powers of evil were themselves judged. Ford, *Gospel of John*, 312–14. Alternatively, Carson argues that the Spirit convicts the world of its sin, its own (false) righteousness, and its own (false) judgment. See Carson, *Jesus*, 138–45.

36. Wright, *Surprised by Scripture*, 196.

37. As Paul expressed it in Phil 3:10–11.

The central elements reflect on the fact that Jesus' disciples will *see* Jesus no more (as he goes to the Father in redeeming death, v. 16, D), but they will later *see* him again (in resurrection). The disciples agitate over what this *seeing* means (vv. 17–19). Their questioning provides the foil by which Jesus could link their *non-seeing* with sadness and their *seeing* with gladness (vv. 20–24, D′).

The third "telling" (vv. 25–27, C′) describes how, until this time, Jesus has spoken only in figures of speech (metaphors). But the use of metaphors will pass when people are able to relate directly with the Father. This leads into the penultimate element (vv. 28–32, B′) that features the Gospel-wide theme that just as Jesus *came from the Father* he is now *going to* him. The disciples claimed to have understood this. Translations vary in the way they present Jesus' response to the disciples' claim that they *believe* (vv. 30–32). As before, the issue of whether people *believe* closes the section. Jesus seems to question whether they *really* believe that he came from the Father—the reality of their believing—as he predicts that they will be scattered, and that he will be alone—albeit with the Father.

The fourth "telling" (v. 33, A′) is the defining sentence of the section. Amidst the disciples' confusion, and anticipating the horror of crucifixion, Jesus says "I have told you this *so that [hina]* you will have peace by being united to me" (GNT). The heart-wrenching drama of the Farewell Discourse (and of all faithful engagement in the suffering love needed in serving God's kingdom) concludes in the assurance of God's peace. We have come to the end of Jesus' conversation with his disciples.

7. JESUS' PRAYER, 17:1–26

Jesus' poignant time with his disciples came to an end with an earnest and intimate prayer to his Father. We might anticipate that it expresses his most heart-felt concerns, and it is full of vital content for us living (as we are) in an often hostile world. And yet there does seem to be an overall chiastic structure to this prayer.

A Way of Reading John's Gospel

But Jesus actually articulated three prayers.[38] The first one expressed the relationship between Jesus and his Father (vv. 1–8). The second was a prayer for his followers, as they sat uncomprehendingly, uneasily, perhaps fearfully, in the room. He begins the prayer, "I pray for them . . ." (vv. 9–19). The third was a prayer for the unseen and uncountable community of believers who would be recruited as Jesus' followers as a result of the witness of the disciples who were present that evening. Thus, Jesus continues, "I pray . . . also for those who believe in me because of their message" (vv. 20–26). We who read that prayer, twenty centuries later, are included within that throng who believe because of the disciples' testimony. Perhaps each of these three prayers also possess some chiastic structure (as suggested later, figs. 38–40).

We may first consider the prayer taken as a whole (fig. 37). Jesus started (vv. 2–3, A) and concluded (vv. 25–26, A') by articulating the vital notion of *knowing God*. Jesus equated the possession of eternal life with a personal knowledge of God and Jesus. This was not an academic knowledge of facts *about* God (which, if such propositions were valid, would be totally beyond human comprehension) but a relational knowledge *with* God (such as any young child can have with his or her mother).

I used to wonder how something as concrete as *life* could be tantamount to the possession of something as intangible as *relationship*. I came to understand that the child-parent connection illustrated this equation. The very structure of a child's developing brain (nerve cells, synapses) is formed by the loving attention of its parents. The physical morphology of the social brain (which can be quantitated and dissected) and its capacity to sustain relationships is formed by love (which is a qualitative attitude of tender care).

---

38. Verney, *Water into Wine*, 177–78; Wright, *John, Part 2*, 90–101.

JOHN 13-17

¹ Jesus' prayer, the hour has come, give glory

A ²⁻³ knowing God, knowing Jesus who was sent
  B ⁴⁻⁵ shown <u>glory</u>—glory <u>before the world was made</u>
    C ⁶⁻⁷ made you <u>known</u> to those out of the <u>world</u>
      D ⁸ I gave them the words you gave me—you sent me
        E ⁹⁻¹⁰ I pray for them—not for the world
          F ¹¹ᵃ I am not, they are in <u>the world</u>
            G ¹¹ᵇ⁻¹² <u>keep them safe</u>; I kept them safe
              H ¹³ I say these things so that [*hina*] they have my joy
            G' ¹⁴⁻¹⁵ <u>keep them safe</u>
          F' ¹⁶⁻¹⁹ I, they do not belong to, are sent into, <u>the world</u>
        E' ²⁰⁻²¹ I pray not only for them—the world will believe
      D' ²² I gave them the glory you gave me—you and I are one
    C' ²³ so that the <u>world</u> may <u>know</u> that you sent me
  B' ²⁴ may see <u>glory</u>—loved <u>before the world was made</u>
A' ²⁵⁻²⁶ knowing God, knowing that Jesus was sent

Figure 37. Jesus' Prayer[39]

Scholarly studies of the effects of childhood neglect (as in poorly resourced orphanages) have enabled the conclusion that "psychosocial deprivation both in institutional and family-based contexts is linked to delays in cognitive, physical and socioemotional development."[40] An impressive demonstration of the role of relationality in forming the structures of life comes from a study of children in neglectful orphanages. Various characteristics were compared for children in long-term institutionalization and those placed into foster families at about two years of age. The fostered children grew bigger, had higher intelligence, and lower rates of mental illness (difficulties with relationships and depression). As

---

39. It goes without saying that this scheme does not capture most of the themes of the prayer, such as the unity of Father, the Son, and the disciples.
40. King et al., "Comprehensive Multilevel Analysis," 573.

they grew into adulthood, the fostered children showed less aggressive behavior.[41]

Knowing is *living*, whether that knowing pertains to vitality and participation in human or in divine society. Interpersonal knowing forms our brains and the personalities to which they give rise. We may accept then that a knowledge of God, as revealed by Jesus, is required for spiritual life, and for socialization into the fellowship of the triune God.

The theme of *knowing* concluded the prayer (vv. 25–26, A'). Jesus knew the Father and had progressively enabled his disciples to grow in this same knowledge. The result was growth in the Father's love and the presence of Jesus' own vitality that came to pervade the lives of his motley group of disciples.

We move on to the second "layer" of Jesus' prayer. Jesus returned to another theme that John has emphasized. Jesus had shown God's *glory*, and he asked that the Father would give him glory in the present, as the time of his obedient sacrifice was upon him (vv. 4–5, B). This is the glory that the divine Son shared with the Father in eternity—*before the world was made*. Jesus completed his prayer by anticipating that his followers—including us in the twenty-first century—would see that glory, which was his from the Father due to the Father's love *before the world was made* (v. 24, B'). Interestingly, Jesus did not petition that his followers would be with him (as we would do when we pray). Rather, he simply expressed his will, his desire, to the Father. As the obedient divine Son, he did not need to request.

Third, Jesus started to address the problem of engagement with the world. His followers were called and came to *know* the Father *out of the world* (vv. 6–7, C). The task given to those same disciples was that of making the Father *known* to the myriad people constituting the unbelieving *world* (v. 23, C').

Fourth, Jesus celebrated his achievement, his transformative influence on the disciples. The elements describe what the Father and he have *given*. He has *given them* the message that God *gave him*, and this message is centered on the claim that the Father sent

---

41. King et al., "Comprehensive Multilevel Analysis," 573–83.

him. The outcome is their faith (v. 8, D). And he has given to his followers *the glory that the Father gave him*, as this is seen in the indivisible unity of Father and Son. The outcome for Jesus' followers is to be their otherworldly unity, modeled on that of Jesus and his Father (v. 22, D').

Fifth, Jesus introduced his prayers for his disciples, both those who were present and those whose obedience was to be in the future. Jesus changed the emphasis from his intimate collaboration with the Father to his care for the assorted men (and women?) in his presence (vv. 9-10, E) and then for the vast number of flawed but redeemed people who, through the future ages of history, would be his emissaries to the world (vv. 20-21, E'). In the first instance, his burden was for his disciples rather than for the world (for which he did not pray). But in the second element his prayer was that through his disciples the world would come to believe.

Jesus emphasized that his disciples remain *in* the world (v. 11a, F), but like him they *did not belong to* the world (vv. 16-19, F'). In their situation of precariousness, of vulnerability, Jesus prayed that they will be kept safe from the world, both from its seductive influences that create divisions (vv. 11b-12, G) and from its outright hostility (vv. 14-15, G'). This remains so urgent for the contemporary Western church, which is thoroughly infiltrated by the values of the world and whose witness is consequently thoroughly compromised.

In this context of looming conflict and alarm, Jesus' central statement—the *hina* statement that defines this seventh and last section of the Farewell Discourse—is that his prayer would lead the disciples to know the joy of Jesus in all its fullness (v. 13, H). Jesus confessed to being troubled (12:27), indeed "deeply troubled" (13:21), but anticipated that his faithful followers will be full of the joy by which he is characterized. This promised state of mind is one that John the author has learned well.[42]

Surprisingly, it may be that each of the three parts of Jesus' prayer shows chiastic structure. Each part of the prayer starts with a statement of the context (vv. 1a, 9, 20) (figs. 38-40). The first

---

42. See also 1 John 1:4 and 2 John 12.

prayer focuses on the relationship of Jesus and the Father (fig. 38). The themes seem to start with what the Father and Jesus have *given* or will *give* (vv. 1b–2, A; v. 8, A'). Jesus spoke of the giving of authority, of eternal life, of those who are true followers, and of God's message. The themes continue with the idea of *knowing* (v. 3, B; v. 7, B') and with what Jesus has *fully achieved in his mission* and what God has *given* (v. 4, C; v. 6, C'). The central element comes back to the request that the Father will reveal the glory of the Son (v. 5a, D)—a glory that is inherently his (v. 5b, D').

1a Setting: Father the hour has come

A **1b-2** Glorify the Son, so that Son may glorify you. <u>You gave him authority</u> over all people, so <u>he might give eternal life</u> to <u>all those you have given him</u>
   B **3** Eternal life is to <u>know</u> you and Jesus Christ
     C **4** <u>I have</u> glorified you, finished work <u>you gave me</u>
       D **5a** Father <u>glorify</u> me in your presence now
       D' **5b** the <u>glory</u> I had with you before the world was
     C' **6** <u>I have</u> made you known to those <u>you gave me</u> out of the world; <u>you gave them to me</u>; they have obeyed your word
   B' **7** now they <u>know</u> that everything you have given me comes from you
A' **8** <u>I gave them</u> <u>the words you gave</u> me; they know that I came from you, believe that you sent me

Figure 38. Jesus' Prayer Regarding the Father and Himself

The prayer for the disciples (fig. 39) commenced with the unity of the Son and the Father and how Jesus' glory was shown through the disciples (v. 10, A). It concluded with the unity of the Son and his followers in their dedication to the Father (v. 19, A'). Jesus had dedicated (consecrated, sanctified) himself to the service of his Father, so that his people would also be dedicated to the work of God. In this he was performing the role of the Jewish high priest.[43] Jesus delivered this "great prayer as the true high priest of God's renewed Israel."[44] For this reason, the prayer of John 17 is often called Jesus' high priestly prayer. Further hints that Jesus is presented as Israel's true high priest were to follow.

⁹ Setting: prayer for his disciples, not the world

A ¹⁰ glory of [Father, Son] shown through the disciples
　B ¹¹ᵃ I am not <u>in the world</u> but they are <u>in the world</u>
　　C ¹¹ᵇ <u>keep them safe</u>, so they may be one
　　　D ¹² <u>I kept them safe, protected them</u>, except one
　　　　E ¹³ I say these things in the world so that [*hina*] they might have my joy
　　　D' ¹⁴ <u>I gave them your word</u>
　　　hated by, don't belong to the world
　　C' ¹⁵ I don't ask you to take them out of the world;
　　I do ask you to <u>keep them safe</u>
　B' ¹⁶⁻¹⁸ I do not belong <u>to the world</u>, just as they do not belong <u>to the world</u>; dedicate them to yourself; I sent them <u>into the world</u>, just as you sent me <u>into the world</u>
A' ¹⁹ dedication of [Son, disciples] to the Father

Figure 39. Jesus' Prayer for the Disciples Then Present

The prayer continued with the fact of disciples' presence *in* the world (v. 11a, B), even as they (with Jesus) did not belong *to* it, and were entrusted with a saving mission *into* it (vv. 16–18, B'). Jesus prayed that the Father would keep them safe (v. 11b, C; v. 15, C'), even as Jesus over the last few years could claim that he had fulfilled the connected tasks of keeping them safe (v. 12, D) and of giving them the Father's message for a hostile world (v. 14, D'). What must be kept safe is "the lasting relationship of mutual trust and love, on both sides of death."[45] This assurance of divine care

---

43. Wright, *John, Part 2*, 96, 100–101.
44. Wright, *John, Part 2*, 104.
45. Ford, *Gospel of John*, 342.

A Way of Reading John's Gospel

in a hostile world culminates in the key *hina* statement that Jesus' words must be the source of their joy (v. 13, E).

Finally, we come to the prayer that envelops all of believing humanity through history. It has been called "the culmination of culminations"—it culminates the Farewell Discourse, which itself culminates the teaching of Jesus, and indeed brings to its culmination: the hope of new covenant elaborated throughout the Hebrew Scriptures (fig. 40).[46]

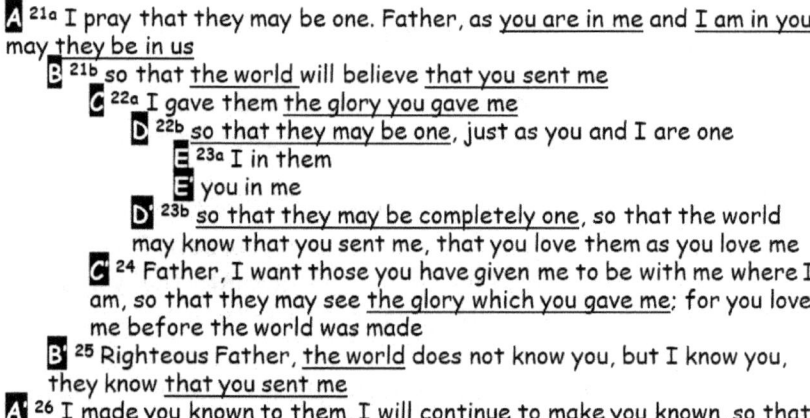

Figure 40. Jesus' Prayer for All Disciples Who Were Still Future

Jesus emphasized the disciples' unity with each other and with the Father and Son. They should be *in* the Father and the Son (v. 21a, A; v. 26, A'), in the same way as the Father and the Son are *in* each other. How can the Father be *in* the Son and the disciples? The eternal life of the triune God is infused into the creatures by the presence of the Holy Spirit. Ford suggests how, to understand this, we could start to meditate along the lines of "mutual

---

46. Ford, *Gospel of John*, 345–46.

glorifying, mutual belonging, and mutual love," and shared joy, truth, and holiness.⁴⁷

Attention is then given to the *world*, that its people will believe that *the Father sent the Son* (v. 21b, B). Even though the *world* does not yet know the Father, the disciples have come to know *the Father sent the Son* (v. 25; B'). The *glory that the Father gave the Son* has been given to the disciples (v. 22a, C) and this same *glory* will be fully visible to the disciples when they finally reside where the Son is (v. 24; C').⁴⁸

The center of this prayer is that the disciples through the ages will be *one*, as the Father and Son are one (v. 22b, D), which is to be *completely one* (v. 23b, D'). This is the wonder of mutual indwelling (v. 23, E, E'). We should grieve that through history Jesus' deepest desire for his followers has been so widely ignored by their fractiousness.

Before leaving Jesus' prayer, two repeated themes could be mentioned. One is the "so that" (*hina*) idea noted above. Jesus' prayer is not merely a series of statements or requests, but expresses the hope that concrete outcomes will follow all that Jesus has achieved. Such outcomes reflect the life-changing dynamic inherent in the Gospel. For example, may believers be united *so that* the world will believe (vv. 21, 23). May believers be with the Son *so that* they may see his glory (v. 24). Jesus has made the Father known *so that* his love may be in them (v. 26).⁴⁹

The other theme is the extraordinary idea that the life and unity of the believer, despite the rough raw material of which they are constituted, are modeled on the life and unity of the triune God. *Just as* it is with Father and Son . . . *so* it is with you.⁵⁰

---

47. Ford, *Gospel of John*, 349.

48. That is, close to the Father's heart (John 1:18); see Ford, *Gospel of John*, 351-52.

49. "So that" (Greek, *hina*) appears in vv. 1, 2, 11, 13 (the defining *hina* statement), 19, 21 (thrice), 22, 23 (twice), 24, and 26.

50. "Just as" (Greek, *kathos*) appears in vv. 11, 14, 16, 18, 21, 22, and 23.

15

JOHN 18-19

Arrest, Trials, and Crucifixion

JESUS AND HIS FRIENDS walked to a loved garden refuge. Jesus was arrested in that place. He was interrogated by the Jewish leaders. Here he faced the hostility of the world in its Jewish manifestation. The identity of the *real high priest* was the issue being adjudicated. Subsequently Jesus was interrogated by the emperor's representative, Pilate. He faced the hostility of the world in its gentile manifestation. The identity of the *real king* was being adjudicated.

ARREST

The arrest of Jesus is described in chiastic form (fig. 41). During this dramatic event, the seventh and final absolute "I am" statement spoken by Jesus is uttered in a particularly emphatic and momentous way.

JOHN 18-19

1-2 After Jesus prayed, he left with his disciples, crossed Kidron Valley to a garden; Jesus and his disciples went in; Judas, the traitor, knew the place—Jesus often met his disciples there

A **3** Judas went to the garden, with Roman soldiers and Temple guards sent by chief priests and Pharisees; carried torches, lanterns, weapons
    B **4a** Jesus knew all that was going to happen to him
        C **4b-5a** came forward and asked:
"Who are your looking for?"
"Jesus of Nazareth," they answered.
"I am he," he said.
            D **5b** Judas, the traitor, was standing there with them
            D' **6** When Jesus said to them, "I am he," they moved back, fell to the ground
        C' **7-8a** Again Jesus asked them,
"Who is it you are looking for?"
"Jesus of Nazareth," they said.
"I told you that I am he," Jesus said.
    B' **8b-9** "If you are looking for me, let these others go"—so what he had said might come true: "I have not lost one of those you gave me"
A' **10-11** Simon Peter had a sword, struck the High Priest's slave (Malchus), cutting off his right ear; Jesus: "Put your sword back in its sheath! Shall I not drink the cup [of suffering] my Father has given me?"

Figure 41. Arrest of Jesus[1]

A brief introduction sets the scene (18:1–2). The outer elements describe the violence of humanity in all its ugliness and futility. The high priest's detachment of men carrying weapons (v. 3, A) and Peter's flailing around with his sword (vv. 10–11, A') are totally incongruous means of dealing with the Prince of Peace who has come to rescue humanity from its savagery by means of his own suffering.

The following nested pair of elements indicate Jesus' control of the situation. They describe his prescience as it related to his own fate (v. 4a, B) and to the fate of his disciples (vv. 8b–9, B').

The central elements focus on Jesus' confession "I am he." As mentioned earlier, Bauckham has indicated that this absolute "I am" saying could simply be taken to mean "I am the man you are looking for." But it could also be understood as the self-designation

---

1. The seventh use of the absolute "I am" saying is found in this pericope. Its three-fold repetition in the central elements (C, C', and D') supports Bauckham's suggestion that it should be taken as an affirmation that Jesus' (divine) nature was shared with YHWH.

of Israel's God. Several lines of evidence support this latter interpretation.

First, the hardened troopers moved back and fell to the ground, in response to "the sheer power of the presence" of the man whom they were to arrest.[2] But there may be irony here: to step back and fall to the ground is "a classic response to divine revelation. . . . The human Jesus of Nazareth [is] at one with the I am of God."[3] The author of the Gospel wants us to see that worship is the appropriate response to this man who identifies himself as "I am." Second, the use of this term in this pericope constitutes the seventh and final time it is used in the Gospel.[4] Third, it is located at the center, the focus, of the chiastic structure (v. 6, D') and it is reiterated in the preceding and succeeding highly parallel elements (vv. 4b–5a, C; vv. 7–8a, C').

TRIAL BEFORE ANNAS AND CAIAPHAS: WHO IS THE REAL HIGH PRIEST?

The next event in the Gospel's narrative is Jesus' trial before the high priest. Annas was not officially the high priest at that time, but he was the power behind the institution. The high priesthood was largely a family dynasty. Following Annas's own tenure, five of his sons took turns to be high priests and the incumbent Caiaphas was his son-in-law.[5] The setting for the action is described (vv. 12–14), and the subsequent account is chiastic in structure (fig. 42).

---

2. Marsh, *Saint John*, 586.
3. Ford, *Gospel of John*, 357–58; see also Wright, *John, Part 2*, 103.
4. Bauckham, *Testimony*, 245.
5. Following Annas, Eleazar (son), Caiaphas (son-in-law), Jonathan, Theophilus, Matthias, and Annas II (all sons), taking us out to the year AD 62; Evans, *Jesus to the Church*, 14.

JOHN 18-19

12-14 Soldiers, Jewish guards arrested Jesus, took him to Annas, father-in-law of Caiaphas, <u>High Priest</u>; Caiaphas had advised Jewish authorities that it was better that one man die for all the people

A **15-17** Simon Peter and another disciple followed Jesus; the other disciple, known to the <u>High Priest</u>, went with Jesus into the courtyard of the <u>High Priest</u>'s house; Peter stayed outside; the other disciple spoke to the girl at the gate, brought Peter in; girl to Peter: "<u>Aren't you also one of the disciples of that man</u>?" Peter: "<u>I am not</u>"
   B **18** servants and guards had a charcoal fire, to keep warm. <u>Peter was standing</u> with them, <u>warming himself</u>
      C **19** <u>High Priest</u> questioned Jesus about his disciples and teaching
         D **20-21** <u>Jesus answered</u>: "I have always spoken publicly to everyone; I always taught in the synagogues and Temple, where all the people come together. I said nothing in secret. Why question me? Question the people who heard me. Ask them what I told them—they know what I said."
           E **22** When Jesus said this, a guard slapped him;
           E' "Is that the way to answer the <u>High Priest</u>?"
         D' **23** <u>Jesus answered</u>: "If I have said anything wrong, tell everyone what it was. But if I spoke the truth, why hit me?"
      C' **24** Annas sent him to Caiaphas, <u>High Priest</u>
   B' **25a** <u>Peter was still standing and warming himself</u>
A' **25b-27** others said to him, "<u>Aren't you also one of the disciples of that man</u>?" Peter denied it: "<u>I am not</u>." One of the <u>High Priest</u>'s slaves, a relative of the man whose ear Peter had cut off: "Didn't I see you with him in the garden?" Peter said "No"—and a rooster crowed

Figure 42. Trial in Annas's House: Who Is the Real High Priest?

The first (18:15-17, A) and last (vv. 25b-27, A') elements describe Peter's stepwise failure to confess his association with Jesus. Common to these elements, Peter denies being Jesus' disciple: "I am not" (v. 17). The second (v. 18, B) and second-to-last (v. 25a, B') elements describe Peter's warming himself by the fire. This was an entirely natural action on a cold night, but it serves as a reminder that when comfort is our own priority, our moral fibre can be compromised.

Annas's actions are summarized (v. 19, C; v. 24, C'), as are Jesus' answers under interrogation (vv. 20-21, D; v. 23, D'). The center of the chiasm (its focus?), strangely, is the slap (v. 22a, E) and reprimand (v. 22b, E') that Jesus received. Perhaps this element is intended to remind readers of the sheer injustice of this (mis)trial of Jesus. Perhaps it is another example of the use of irony that pervades John's Gospel. This pericope alludes to the high priest many times—in the introductory section, in the paired elements A and A', C and C', and in the central focus (E'). Might it be possible that here the author is comparing the corrupt, worldly high priesthood, in all its extortionate cupidity and nepotistic thirst for power, with the true high priest who rightly reveals God to humanity? The unspoken, alternative true high priest is in fact Jesus.

In this Gospel, Jesus has been presented as the true Lamb or sacrifice, the true Bread from heaven, the true Temple. Does this otherwise sordid scene lead us to recognise that he is the one true high priest (as is implied in his prayer in chapter 17)? It is Jesus alone who is the point in whom God and his creatures interact.

TRIAL BEFORE PILATE: WHO IS THE REAL KING?

The narrative progresses to Jesus' trial before the Roman prefect Pontius Pilate. There is evidence that Pilate's actions were generally directed to the promotion of the Roman religion, and in particular to fostering the imperial cult. As such, he was a representative of the emperor and the worship ascribed to him in the province of Judea.[6] This was truly a clash of the kingdoms.

Scholars have intimated that the trial of Jesus before Prefect Pilate is presented as an extensive chiasm.[7] This chiastic unit extends across the boundary between chapters 18 and 19. I have sought to reconstruct it, as shown below (fig. 43). In general, the paralleled elements represent contributions from each of the three voices in the court scene. For example, the second (18:29, B) and penultimate (19:16a, B′) elements feature Pilate. In the former case he asks for the charge against Jesus; in the latter case, he pronounces the sentence. The conversation partners are Pilate, the Jewish authorities, and of course Jesus, whose contribution to the trial proceedings is limited but seminally important. Jesus' speech (and in one case, his refusal to answer) is reported in only 18:34 and in two pairs of elements (18:36, H; 19:11, H′; and 18:37b, J; 19:9b, J′).

---

6. Taylor, "Pontius Pilate," 555–82.

7. As noted earlier, see du Rand, *Johannine Perspectives*, 21; Kim, *Sourcebook*, 14.

JOHN 18-19

Figure 43. Trial Before Prefect Pilate: Who Is the Real King?

In the first doublet, Jesus speaks of his own kingdom (18:36, H) and of Pilate's imperial authority, which is in reality given by God (19:11, H'). Jesus here reveals himself to be the judge representing the higher authority. The confrontation between Jesus and Pilate comprises the "ultimate showdown" between the kingdoms of God and of Caesar.[8] Regarding his kingdom, Jesus says that it does not belong to this world; that is, it is not *from* or *out of* the

8. Wright, *God Became King*, 229-30.

corrupt power plays of humanity, although it is resoundingly *in* and *for* this world, in all its desperate need. In fact, it is constituted by peace, not violence. Jesus' crucifixion is *what has to happen* if God's kingdom is to be established by nonviolent means.[9]

In the other paired parallel involving Jesus' speech, Pilate questioned him about his *kingship*, which Jesus had affirmed. However, Jesus expressed that kingship in terms of his *coming* to witness to the truth (18:37b–38a, J). Again, Jesus' dealings with Pilate represent a conflict of the kingdoms: "The difference between the kingdoms is striking. Caesar's kingdom (and all other kingdoms that originate in the world) make their way by fighting. But Jesus' kingdom—God's kingdom enacted through Jesus—makes its way with quite a different weapon, one that Pilate refuses to acknowledge: telling the truth."[10] This truth includes the fact that Jesus was going to die in place of the guilty—as his substitution for Barabbas on the gibbet was going to make clear. In the parallel element (19:7–9, J'), the same issues are raised again by the people ("he claimed to be the Son of God," that is, to be *king*) and Pilate (from whence do you *come*?). However, in this case Jesus remained silent. Presumably he saw no need to repeat himself in the face of willful, stubborn resistance.

The tragedy for the Jewish leaders is that their grasping after political power led them to reject the creed of their devout forebears. It was the latter who suffered and died by the principle "We have no king but God." But now, in their determination to rid themselves of Jesus, the authorities perversely inverted the statement of loyalty: "We have no king but Caesar" (19:15c, C').[11] The priests have rejected their God. Pilate the judge has rejected truth. That is the price of compromise.[12]

David Bentley Hart argues that this scene depicts the most far-reaching revolution of thought and value in all of human

---

9. Wright, *John, Part 2*, 114–15; Wright, *God Became King*, 230.
10. Wright, *God Became King*, 144–45.
11. Wright, *God Became King*, 146.
12. Wright, *John, Part 2*, 124.

history.[13] The figure of Jesus represented the oppressed slave class, faceless, deemed contemptible and indeed ridiculous in the eyes of the elite. Pilate represented power, privilege, and the unquestionable authority of the gods (who "love order above all else") and of empire. Hart writes that the Gospel of John "approaches the confrontation between Christ and Pilate from a vantage unprecedented in human culture: the faith of Easter." God does not approve of "the verdict of his alleged earthly representatives" such as Pilate. The surprising truth is that God "vindicates and restores to life the very man they have 'justly' condemned." The glory of God is revealed in a condemned man representing the masses on the underside of history. It is the proud and mighty who are absurd; and "the figure of Christ seems only to grow in dignity."[14] This encounter reveals the divine image in every person; it is the origin of human rights, of the recognition of the dignity of all people.

The crux of the chiasm might be expected to provide the key point of this torrid encounter. And it quotes the protestation of the presiding judge. Pilate declared that Jesus is innocent (19:4, O).[15] John wants us to know that Jesus was the perfect, unblemished Passover sacrifice. To emphasize this, Pilate restated Jesus' innocence in paralleled elements: "I cannot find any reason to condemn him" (18:38b, K; 19:6b, K'). To emphasize that Jesus was the true Lamb, John's Gospel states that it was almost noon on the day before Passover, "about the sixth hour" (19:14), the time when the Passover lambs were killed.[16] This hour of sacrifice has been anticipated through the Gospel. When Jesus and the author's commentary in John's Gospel have spoken of Jesus' "hour," his death has been in mind.[17]

13. Everyone should read the chapter titled "The Face of the Faceless" in Hart, *Atheist Delusions*, 166–82.

14. Hart, *Atheist Delusions*, 173–74.

15. This is not the only time Pilate speaks a profound truth; he later declares Jesus to be the King of the Jews (19:19).

16. Ford, *Gospel of John*, 373.

17. Ford, *Gospel of John*, 63; for "hour," see John 2:4, 7:30, 8:20; for references to the "hour" as it approached, see 12:23, 27; 13:1; 17:1; for a reference to the "hour" having arrived, see 19:14.

A WAY OF READING JOHN'S GOSPEL

The narrative proceeds to the crucifixion of Jesus (fig. 44). As is typical of the Gospel, there is a brief summary statement of the event (19:17–18). The four words embedded in this must be the most surprising, incomprehensible, and paradoxical in all of literature: "There they crucified him." *There* referred to Jerusalem, the city of David, the site of the temple, the place where heaven and earth met, and where God's purposes were to be fulfilled. *They* were the chosen people with a two-thousand-year history of engagement with YHWH. *Crucified* refers to a particularly savage and humiliating execution—and associated in the Jewish mind with God's curse.[18] And *him* refers to the teacher of love, justice, and peace—the good shepherd, the true vine, the Son.

```
17-18 Setting: He carried his cross to "The Place of the Skull/Golgotha;" they crucified him and two others

 A  19 Pilate wrote a notice, had it put on the cross
     B  "Jesus of Nazareth, King of the Jews"
        C  20 Many people read it—the place where Jesus was crucified was near the city
        C  notice was written in Hebrew, Latin, Greek
     B  21 chief priests: "Do not write 'King of the Jews,' but 'This man said, I am King of the Jews'"
 A  22 Pilate: "What I have written stays written"

 A  23-24 soldiers crucified Jesus, divided his clothes, his robe was seamless, they threw dice for it; to make
    the scripture come true: "They divided my clothes among themselves, gambled for my robe"
     B  25-27 near Jesus' cross: mother, mother's sister, Mary wife of Clopas, Mary of Magdala; Jesus
        saw mother and the disciple he loved; to his mother, "This is your son;" to the disciple, "This is your
        mother;" the disciple took her home
        C  28-30 Jesus knew everything had been completed; to make scripture come true: "I am thirsty;"
           sponge soaked in wine lifted to his lips; Jesus drank: "It is finished!"
           D  bowed his head, gave up his spirit
              E  31 Jewish authorities to Pilate: break the legs of the men who had been crucified,
                 take the bodies down from crosses
                 F  because it was Friday; did not want bodies on crosses on the Sabbath,
                 F  the coming Sabbath was especially holy
              E  32 soldiers broke the legs of the men who had been crucified with Jesus
           D  33 Jesus was dead, did not break his legs
        C  34 soldier pierced Jesus' side with a spear, blood and water poured out
     B  35 The one who saw this has testified, so that you may believe; what he said is true, he knows that
        he speaks the truth
 A  36-37 to make the scripture come true: "Not one of his bones will be broken;" scripture: "People will look
    at him whom they pierced"
```

Figure 44. Crucifixion (First Phase of Sign 7)

A mini-chiasm seems to follow. The *titulus* was Prefect Pilate's handiwork (v. 19a, A; v. 22, A′). The specific accusation,

---

18. Deut 21:22–23.

unpalatable to the Jewish authorities, was that Jesus was the King of the Jews (v. 19b, B; v. 21, B'). The notice was witnessed by the crowds who walked by (v. 20a, C). It was written in the languages of the devout (Hebrew), the powerful (Latin), and of the marketplace (Greek, v. 20b, C'). The use of three languages provides a hint of universality regarding the significance of this terrible event.[19] John's Gospel is announcing that Jesus is Israel's Messiah who has been sent to the whole world.[20]

The main account starts (vv. 23-24, A)[21] and finishes (vv. 36-37, A') with appeals to Scripture.[22] The allusion to Ps 22 directs the reader to Jesus as the righteous sufferer, "the one through whose shameful death the weight of Israel's sin, and behind that the sin of the whole world, is being dealt with."[23]

The ensuing nested pair of elements (vv. 25-27, B; v. 35, B') describe Jesus' associates—especially the anonymous disciple, the trustworthy eyewitness of this momentous event. Attention changes to Jesus: the source of living water was himself thirsty, but he had victoriously completed his mission (vv. 28-30a, C); and blood and water poured out of him, signifying both his redemptive sacrifice and the cleansing of people's hearts (v. 34, C'). He had indeed died (v. 30b, D; v. 33, D'), and the breaking of his legs to hasten death was not needed (v. 31a, E; v. 32, E'). This is a significant

---

19. Barclay indicated that the Hebrews taught the world the worship of the true God, Rome taught the world law, and Greece taught the world beauty of form and of thought. But in Jesus people could see the very image of God, the true law and kingdom of God, and the supreme beauty and highest thought of God. "The consummation of all these things is seen in Jesus." Barclay, *Gospel of John*, 2:293.

20. Wright, *John, Part 2*, 126.

21. Verse 23 indicates that Jesus' robe (GNT; tunic, RSV; undergarment, JB, NIV; shirt, JBP) was one woven piece, without seams, as was the high priest's robe. Is this a further allusion to Jesus' high priesthood, as suggested also from the description of his appearance before Annas, the usurping high priest? Barclay, *Gospel of John*, 2:296.

22. Ps 22:18 and Zech 12:10, respectively.

23. Wright, *John, Part 2*, 127.

piece of information, for the Hebrew Scriptures stipulate that the bones of the Passover lamb were not to be broken.[24]

The center of the cruciform indicates that the great redemptive task was done as Sabbath rest was coming (v. 31b, F). But this Passover Sabbath was especially holy (v. 31c, F'). Again, irony prevails. It was not the conjunction of two ancient rituals, but the advent of the new exodus, God's Sabbath rest, that had arrived. The cost of new creation, written into history from before the beginning, had been paid.

The story is completed with a description of how Joseph of Arimathea and Nicodemus placed the body of Jesus in a nearby rock tomb. This was an action of great commitment because handling a dead body would have excluded them from the activities of the Passover celebration. Bauckham has suggested that an ancient Jewish tradition that speaks of five disciples of Jesus contained a garbled reference to Nicodemus.[25] The massive amount of myrrh and aloes used to embalm the body of Jesus is a pointer to royalty, the kingship of Jesus.[26]

---

24. Exod 12:46; Num 9:12; Ps 34:20; Barclay, *Gospel of John*, 2:303-4; Marsh, *Saint John*, 621; Ford, *Gospel of John*, 389.

25. Disciples of Jesus were said to include Naqqai (a diminutive form of Naqdimon) and Bumi (a name from the Ben Gurion / Naqdimon family); see Bauckham, *Testimony*, 167-70.

26. Ford, *Gospel of John*, 370.

16

JOHN 20

Resurrection and Divine Vindication

JOHN'S GOSPEL REPORTS THE world-transforming event of the resurrection of Jesus, which completes the seventh of Jesus' signs.[1] We have already noted that when the powers-that-be asked Jesus to provide a sign of his authority, he told them of the rebuilding of the temple, by which he referred to his own body.[2] The sign was his resurrection. In addition, at the end of chapter 20, which describes the first witnesses to Jesus' resurrection, the text continues, "Jesus performed many other signs that are not written in this book" (20:30). Those *other* unrecorded signs must be additional to that *sign* just recounted, the resurrection.[3]

The disciples discovered the tomb had been vacated. Jesus met and conversed with his disciples. In John 20 these encounters seem to fall into two pairs of chiastic structures (four in all). In many ways they are parallel stories in which the second goes beyond the first in its theological content.

---

1. The resurrection occurred on Sunday morning, the third day (John 20:1). Verney stated that John had been preparing his readers for this: the first and final signs, pointing to transformation of the world, featured the third day (2:1, 2:19), as did the nested second and sixth signs, pointing to Jesus' authority over life and death (4:43, 11:6). See Verney, *Water into Wine*, 193.

2. John 2:18–22; Rae, "To Render Praise," 201–20.

3. John 20:30; Harris, *Raised*, 29.

A Way of Reading John's Gospel

The outermost pair of elements features Mary of Magdala. The setting is the first day of the week, symbolizing the advent, the inauguration, of the new creation.[4] The first part of the story is formed as a chiasm probably because it reflects the way the drama unfolds (fig. 45). The episode proceeds through Mary (A elements), the male disciples (B elements), the anonymous disciple (C elements), and the burial clothes that had enshrouded the body of Jesus (D elements).

At the start of the story Mary is presented in a state of confusion if not dismay (vv. 1–2, A). At the end of the story, she was still giving vent to her grief (v. 11a, A'). There has been little change in her state of mind.

1a Setting: early on Sunday morning

A **1b-2** <u>Mary</u> of Magdala went to the <u>tomb</u>, saw that the stone had been taken away; ran to Simon Peter and the other disciple whom Jesus loved: "They have taken the Lord from the tomb, we don't know where they have put him!"
   B **3** Peter and the other <u>disciple went</u> to the tomb
      C **4-5** <u>the other disciple</u> ran faster than Peter, <u>reached the tomb first</u>; <u>saw</u> the linen cloths, <u>did not go in</u>
         D **6-7** Simon Peter went into the tomb, saw the <u>linen cloths</u> lying there
         D' and the cloth which had been around Jesus' head, not with the <u>linen cloths</u>, rolled up by itself
      C' **8-9** <u>the other disciple</u>, who had <u>reached the tomb first</u>, <u>went in</u>; he <u>saw</u>, believed, did not understand the scripture which said [Jesus] must rise from death
   B' **10** <u>disciples went</u> home
A' **11a** <u>Mary</u> stood crying outside the <u>tomb</u>

Figure 45. Mary Discovers the Empty Tomb (Second Phase of Sign 7)

In response to Mary's report, Peter and that mysterious anonymous disciple (the eyewitness author?) hurried to the tomb (v.

---

4. Wright, *John, Part 2*, 2:140, 149.

3, B) and, in response to what they have observed, retraced their steps back home (v. 10, B'). The anonymous disciple reached the tomb first (vv. 4–5, C) and eventually went in (vv. 8–9, C'). The account emphasizes what he *saw*, and he is said to *believe*. But what did he believe? That the body of Jesus had gone (as Mary said)? That Jesus had returned to his Father (as Jesus had said he would)?[5] Many scholars suggest that what this disciple believed was that Jesus had risen[6]—but the comment that the disciples as yet failed to "understand the scripture" (20:9 GNT)[7] indicates that their faith was not integrated into an informed understanding of what God was really doing, that is, of *resurrection*. Our faith is always imperfect, developing.

At the center of the chiasm (vv. 6–7, D, D') we find Peter barging into the tomb, and we are told of how the empty gravecloths were arranged. This is important information for a later fully fledged understanding of the transformation of Jesus' body.[8] Resurrection is implied but it all seems to be rather understated. The male disciples seem to have undergone no great change in their state of mind. There seems to be nothing to get excited about. There is no climax. They trudge home, presumably to the (Jerusalem) residence where Peter was staying with the beloved disciple.

The second part of Mary's discovery (fig. 46) is altogether different. It starts with Mary's brokenness (vv. 11b-13, A) and finishes with her confident, excited, joyful report that she has encountered Jesus (v. 18, A'). Talk about sadness to gladness!

---

5. Ford, *Gospel of John*, 397.

6. For example, Wright, *John, Part 2*, 141–42.

7. The relevant scripture probably being Ps 16:10–11; see Harris, *Raised*, 27–28; Ford, *Gospel of John*, 397.

8. "Apparently the resurrection had occurred by Jesus' passing through his burial garments." Harris, *Raised*, 27.

A ¹¹ᵇ⁻¹³ As she wept, she looked in the tomb, saw two angels, sitting where Jesus' body had been, one at the head, the other at the feet: "Woman, why are you crying?" She answered, "They have taken my Lord away, and I do not know where they have put him!"
 B ¹⁴⁻¹⁵ᵃ she turned, saw Jesus; did not know that it was Jesus. Jesus: "Woman, why are you crying? Who are you looking for?"
  C ¹⁵ᵇ She thought he was the gardener: "Sir, if you took him away, tell me where you have put him; I will get him."
   D ¹⁶ᵃ Jesus said to her, "Mary!"
  C ¹⁶ᵇ She turned and said "Rabboni!" ("Teacher")
 B ¹⁷ Jesus: "Do not hold on to me, because I have not yet gone back to the Father. But go to my brothers and tell them that I am returning to my Father and your Father, my God and your God."
A ¹⁸ Mary of Magdala went and told the disciples that she had seen the Lord and that he had said these things to her.

Figure 46. Jesus Appears to Mary of Magdala

The next pair of elements describes the approach of Jesus to Mary (vv. 14–15a, B) and then his assurance to her of his imminent return to his Father and God—who had now become theirs too (v. 17, B′). Wright says, "A new relationship has sprung to life.... The disciples are welcomed into a new world" where they are enabled to be "true Israelites at last."[9] Mary had changed from puzzlement (v. 15b, C) to joyful recognition (v. 16b, C′).

The center of the paragraph provides the reason for the abrupt change in mood. Jesus said one word: Mary (v. 16a, D)! Wright makes the point that in John's Gospel, Mary of Magdala is generally called by the Greek form of her name, Maria (20:1, 11). But when she meets Jesus in resurrection, he addresses her by her Hebrew name, Mariam or Miriam, the name her mother would have given her. The risen Jesus endows upon this woman her true identity.[10] She knows she is loved, valued, secure, and called into joyful relation with the living Messiah.

Chapter 20 continues with the encounter of Jesus with the apostles. They have heard Mary's excited report but are evidently

---

9. Wright, *John, Part 2*, 145.
10. Wright, *Surprised by Scripture*, 216.

JOHN 20

unimpressed. They too must meet Jesus before they take this resurrection story seriously.

The first meeting is without Thomas (fig. 47). It describes an encounter and the disciples' *seeing* of the living Jesus. It describes their deep visceral joy. It is a very human account of a reunion. But *believing* is not mentioned. The second event has Thomas present (fig. 48). It goes beyond the mere event and the disciples' seeing. It is not about the feeling of joy but about a disciple's rational and heart-felt *worship*. It is not about a local reunion but about the universality of the need for saving faith. *Believing* is repeatedly emphasized.

The first pericope (fig. 47) starts with the disciples' fear as they hide (v. 19a, A) and ends with the promise of the Spirit's power and the commission to engage the world with the offer of God's forgiveness (vv. 22-23, A'). Jesus breathed on his disciples in the same way as God breathed into human beings the breath (or spirit) of life in the Genesis creation story.[11] This signifies new life, a new humanity, a new creation. The disciples were given a new commission to announce, to be agents of, God's offer of forgiveness to the world.

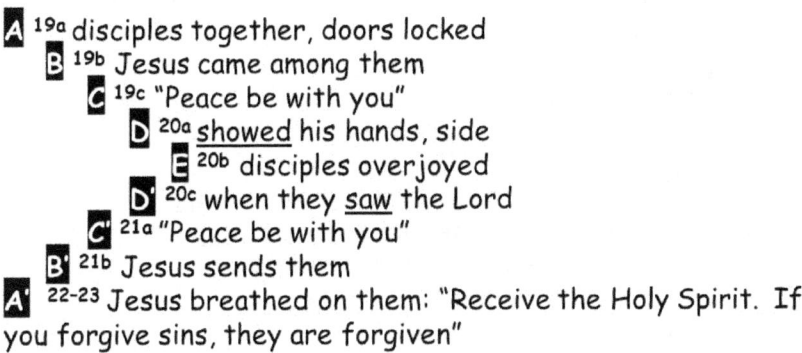

A 19a disciples together, doors locked
  B 19b Jesus came among them
    C 19c "Peace be with you"
      D 20a <u>showed</u> his hands, side
        E 20b disciples overjoyed
      D' 20c when they <u>saw</u> the Lord
    C' 21a "Peace be with you"
  B' 21b Jesus sends them
A' 22-23 Jesus breathed on them: "Receive the Holy Spirit. If you forgive sins, they are forgiven"

Figure 47. Particularity of History: Disciples *See* and Express *Joy*

---

11. Gen 2:7. "The disciples receive the Spirit of the crucified and risen Jesus, infusing them with the reality of his life, death, and resurrection, inspiring them to be sent as he was sent." Ford, *Gospel of John*, 405.

A Way of Reading John's Gospel

The next pair of elements describes how Jesus came among them in their fear (v. 19b, B) and then sent them out into the world (v. 21b, B′) in the confidence that God's kingdom had been established in power. Jesus greeted and blessed them using the standard parlance—*shalom* if he was speaking in Hebrew (v. 19c, C; v. 21a, C′).

The crux of the paragraph is about Jesus *showing* his scars to them (v. 20a, D), and their *seeing* him (v. 20c, D′). This visual evidence elicits exuberant joy (v. 20b, E). It is a very predictable human scene. Here is the "sadness to *joy*" of which Jesus spoke during the Farewell Discourse.[12] But faith does not feature in this current paragraph. From all we have learned in John's Gospel, the story is far from complete.

The second pericope (fig. 48) describes the next meeting a week later. Thomas was present. There are marked parallels between the two pericopes. Elements A–D describe the same sequence of events (compare figs. 47 and 48). The disciples were huddled behind lock doors. Jesus appeared. He pronounced his peace upon them. He showed them his scars.

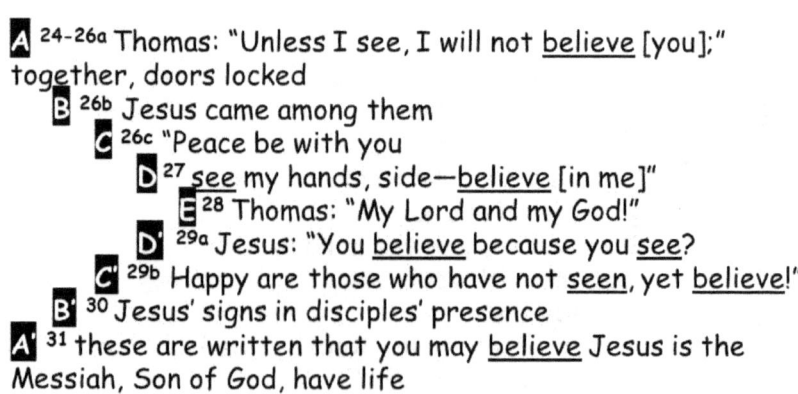

Figure 48. Universality of Gospel: All Who *Believe* in Jesus' Deity Are *Blessed*

---

12. Cf. John 16:20–22 and 20:20b.

The great difference between the pericopes is that the second featured the imperative of *believing*. It was Thomas who introduced the word *believe*. Before Jesus appeared, Thomas stated that he would not believe the report of his fellow disciples (vv. 24–25, A).[13] Subsequently, Jesus himself raised the idea of believing (v. 27, D; v. 29a, D′) but in a different sense to that used by Thomas. The issue was *not* now believing a report that Jesus is alive—that had become obvious to Thomas, as Jesus stood before him. The fact of Jesus' resurrection no longer needed faith.[14]

Rather, Jesus challenged Thomas to believe in the *significance*, the *implications*, of the resurrection. What did it indicate about Jesus himself? In v. 27 (D), he invited Thomas to *see* his scars and to *believe* in who he (Jesus) is. But in v. 29 (D′), Jesus indicated that it will be necessary to believe (again, in who he is) *without seeing*.

At the crux of this chiasm (the fifth element), Thomas worshiped. He declared that Jesus was his Lord and God (v. 28, E).[15] Thomas expressed more than mere joyful emotion: his faith evinced interpretation, perception, understanding, a change in his deepest loyalties. This is the climax of John's Gospel. The confession of Thomas is what John hoped would be expressed by all his readers.[16] It is a basis of the church's conviction that Jesus shares in the divine identity. Thomas's statement had "the silence of consent."[17] What Thomas said was entirely appropriate, because Jesus accepted his devotion.

The title "Our Lord and God" (*Dominus et Deus Noster*) was a title used in the imperial cult. It was initiated by Emperor Domitian (who reigned AD 81–96). The declaration of Thomas, and of all those who recognise Jesus' divine holiness on the basis of his

---

13. Ford, *Gospel of John*, 409.

14. And Jesus' appearance to the disciples the second time assures the reader of the Gospel that the disciples' testimony is to be trusted; Ford, *Gospel of John*, 409.

15. Wright, *Resurrection*, 668.

16. Wenham and Walton, *Exploring*, 258.

17. Thurmer, *Son*, 50.

resurrection,[18] was to be an explicit challenge to self-aggrandizing Roman emperors from the end of the first century to the beginning of the fourth—and indeed to all of history's despots.[19]

Jesus changed his greeting of peace (v. 26c, C) to a benediction (v. 29b, C′): how blessed, how fortunate are all those who believe (in his total vindication by the Father) without seeing him or his physical scars. Jesus was looking beyond the men in the room to the millions of people through the ages who would trust in his divine saving work.

The conclusion of the story contains the expected invitation to all readers and hearers to believe in Jesus (v. 31, A′). The world has come a long way since Thomas's guarded scepticism at the commencement of this short story (vv. 24–26a, A).

---

18. Rom 1:4.
19. Ford, *Gospel of John*, 412.

17

JOHN 21

Commissioning of Peter and the Beloved Disciple

THIS LAST CHAPTER OF John's Gospel presents Jesus and a group of his disciples back in Galilee, on the shore of a lake. It is an integral part of the book, an epilogue if you like, to balance the prologue (1:1– 18).[1]

The main story (vv. 1–14) sets out to emphasise again the disciples' encounter with Jesus following his resurrection (fig. 49). It tells us of the power of God to provide necessities when human resources are inadequate. It is also commissioning time. The Synoptic Gospels describe Jesus' call of the disciples to be fishermen who will catch people. This occurs at the beginning of their stories, the inception of Jesus' work.[2] Jesus' call of Andrew, Peter, Philip, Nathaniel, and the one significant anonymous disciple are described in John 1, but John seems to keep the "fisherman" metaphor for the end of his narrative, the inception of the church's work. The miraculous catch of fish "is to depict symbolically the church's mission of bringing people to faith in Jesus and new life as children of God."[3]

---

1. Bauckham, *Testimony*, 271–78.
2. Mark 1:17, Matt 4:19, Luke 5:10.
3. Bauckham, *Testimony*, 281.

A Way of Reading John's Gospel

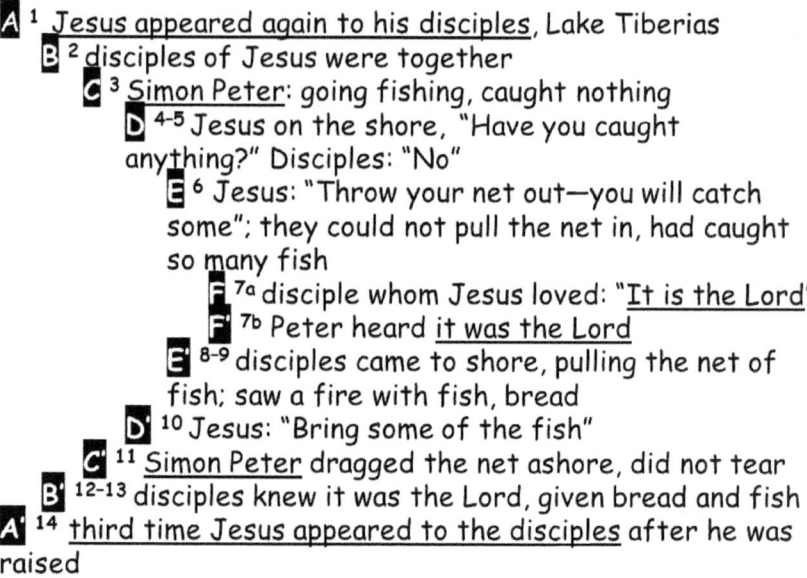

Figure 49. Breakfast on the Beach: "It Is the Lord!"

The first (v. 1, A) and last (v. 14, A') elements provide essentially the same information. This lakeside episode was another occasion when the risen Jesus appeared to his disciples.

The second (v. 2, B) and penultimate (vv. 12–13, B') elements feature the disciples, but there is a progression in their togetherness. In the earlier element, they seem to be in some sort of limbo. In the absence of a specific directive, they returned to secular work. It is well known that Peter and the sons of Zebedee (the only time the brothers are mentioned in this Gospel) were hardcore fishermen. At the end of the story, the disciples had become united in their recognition that this figure on the shore was in fact Jesus himself. In that perception, Jesus fed them with bread and fish—an echo of the way he fed the crowd and spoke of himself as the living bread that come from heaven,[4] of the two disciples at Emmaus

---

4. See especially John 6:48, 51.

JOHN 21

who recognized Jesus when he broke bread,[5] and of the Lord's Supper, the eucharistic celebration,[6] of which the bread and wine remain for many of Jesus' followers the richly allusive designated icons of their Lord.

The third element from each end features Peter, the leader of the group to whom the other disciples looked for direction. In the first element (v. 3, C) he led the group in a fruitless fishing exercise. In the corresponding element (v. 11, C'), Peter delivered the huge catch consequent upon obedience to Jesus' instruction. The group of disciples shared in this transformation from failure (vv. 4–6a, D) to abundance (v. 10, D').

The center of the story repeats the information describing the astonishing weight of the catch (v. 6b, E; v. 8, E'), and focuses on the conclusion that the stranger who made it all possible was the Lord, emphasized by a direct parallelism (v. 7a, F; v. 7b, F').

Following this fishing narrative, Jesus and Peter engage in conversation. Jesus has made a charcoal fine (21:9), reminiscent of the charcoal fire beside which Peter fearfully dissociated himself from Jesus (cf. 18:18, 25–27). Painful memories of failure by one charcoal fire were recalled and forgiven, in a loving encounter by another.[7] Peter had failed three times and now Jesus gave him three opportunities to confess his love for Jesus. Ford notes that, in this Gospel, a loving response to Jesus is never taken for granted, but when Jesus asked Peter, "Do you love me?," a decision to love him was required.[8] The Gospel of John presents the same question to all of us.

The final anecdote in the Gospel represents the author's signing off. He both presents himself as the ideal witness, and also corrects a rumor that was spreading misinformation through the early church community (fig. 50).

---

5. Luke 24:30–31, 35.
6. Mark 14:22–24, Matt 26:26–28, Luke 22:17–20, 1 Cor 11:23–25.
7. Wright, *John, Part 2*, 158–59; Ford, *Gospel of John*, 420.
8. Cf. John 14:15, 23, 24, 28; 15:10; Ford, *Gospel of John*, 424.

A ²⁰ Peter saw the disciple whom Jesus loved, who had leaned close to Jesus
  B ²¹ Peter: "what about this man?"
    C ²² Jesus: "<u>If I want him to live until I come, what is that to you?</u> Follow me!"
      D ²³ a rumor spread: <u>this disciple would not die</u>
      D' Jesus did not say <u>he would not die</u>
    C' [Jesus]: "<u>If I want him to live until I come, what is that to you?</u>"
  B' ²⁴ He is the disciple who testified, wrote these things
A' we know that his testimony is true

Figure 50. The Ideal Witness Signs Off

Peter is used to turn the spotlight onto this mysterious unnamed disciple "whom Jesus loved" (v. 20, A). Why is this man haunting the text? The final phrase (v. 24b, A') leaves us with the assurance that his report on Jesus (what we call *John's Gospel*) is trustworthy. The disciple whom Jesus loved presents himself (as Bauckham argues strongly) as the ideal witness.

Peter's question regarding this man (v. 21, B) and its parallel (v. 24a, B') emphasise the same point. Who is this man? He is the author, the ideal and trustworthy witness.[9]

The center of the chiasm disposes of a misunderstanding. Jesus rebutted Peter's nosey question with the hypothetical case "If I want him to live until I come . . ." (v. 22). It was not Peter's business to know the Lord's purpose for that other disciple (v. 22, C; v. 23c, C'). Jesus never said that the disciple would live until he (Jesus) returned (as stipulated in the direct parallelism of v. 23a). One imagines that the story has been penned when "the disciple whom Jesus loved" is old, is approaching death, wants to lay a potentially harmful rumor to rest, and is saying goodbye. He leaves his readers with two thoughts. He is a trustworthy witness. His

---

9. Bauckham, *Eyewitnesses*, 390–402; *Testimony*, 85–91.

death is of no particular significance as regards the timing of the Lord's return.

This disciple is also an example for us. The Lord will not arrange his schedule according to our preferences, the fate of the stock market, or the terrors of war, climate change, or social upheaval. We are left with the imperative of providing trustworthy and faithful testimony to the glory of God and to his salvation as revealed in his eternal Son. Let us serve unstintingly as we wait for the consummation of God's project: "Even so, come Lord Jesus!"

BIBLIOGRAPHY

Bailey, Kenneth. *Jesus through Middle Eastern Eyes*. Downers Grove, IL: InterVarsity, 2008.
———. *Paul through Mediterranean Eyes*. Downers Grove, IL: InterVarsity, 2011.
Barclay, William. *The Gospel of John*. Vol. 1. Edinburgh: Saint Andrew, 1955.
———. *The Gospel of John*. Vol. 2. Edinburgh: Saint Andrew, 1956.
Bauckham, Richard. *Jesus: A Very Short Introduction*. Oxford: Oxford University Press, 2011.
———. *Jesus and the Eyewitnesses*. Grand Rapids: Eerdmans, 2006.
———. *The Testimony of the Beloved Disciple*. Grand Rapids: Baker, 2007.
Biblical Archaeology Society. "The Siloam Pool: Where Jesus Healed the Blind Man." Bible History Daily, July 4, 2024. https://www.biblicalarchaeology.org/daily/biblical-sites-places/biblical-archaeology-sites/the-siloam-pool-where-jesus-healed-the-blind-man/.
Brouwer, Wayne. "Understanding Chiasm and Assessing Macro-Chiasm as a Tool of Biblical Interpretation." *Calvin Theological Journal* 53 (2018) 99–127.
Bultmann, Rudolph. *The Gospel of John: A Commentary*. Philadelphia: Westminster, 1971.
Burge, Gary. "A Specific Problem in the New Testament Text and Canon: The Woman Caught in Adultery (John 7:53–8:11)." *Journal of the Evangelical Theological Society* 27.2 (1984) 141–48.
Burridge, Richard A. *What Are the Gospels?* 2nd ed. Grand Rapids: Eerdmans, 2004.
Carson, Donald A. *Jesus and His Friends: His Farewell Message and Prayer in John 14 to 17*. Leicester: Inter-Varsity, 1980.
City of David. "The Ancient Siloam Pool in the City of David National Park in Jerusalem Will Be Fully Excavated and Opened to the General Public." Archaeology. https://cityofdavid.org.il/en/siloam-pool-opened-eng/.
Douglas, J. D., et al., eds. *The Illustrated Bible Dictionary*. Leicester: Inter-Varsity, 1980.

Bibliography

du Rand, Jan A. *Johannine Perspectives: Introduction to the Johannine Writings.* Part 1. Johannesburg: Orion, 1997.

Evans, Craig A. *From Jesus to the Church.* Louisville: Westminster John Knox, 2014.

———. *Jesus and His World: The Archaeological Evidence.* London: SPCK, 2012.

Ford, David F. *The Gospel of John: A Theological Commentary.* Grand Rapids: Baker, 2021.

Grabiner, Steven. "*Pericope Adulterae*: A Most Perplexing Passage." *Andrews University Seminary Studies* 56 (2018) 91–114.

Harris, Murray J. *Raised Immortal.* Basingstoke, UK: Marshall, Morgan & Scott, 1983.

Hart, David Bentley. *Atheist Delusions: The Christian Revolution and Its Fashionable Enemies.* New Haven: Yale University Press, 2009.

Kim, Sang-Hoon. *Sourcebook of the Structures and Styles in John 1–10.* Eugene, OR: Wipf & Stock, 2014.

King, Lucy S., et al. "A Comprehensive Multilevel Analysis of the Bucharest Early Intervention Project: Causal Effects on Recovery from Early Severe Deprivation." *American Journal of Psychiatry* 180.8 (2023) 573–83.

Koester, Craig. R. "'The Savior of the World' (John 4:42)." *Journal of Biblical Literature* 109.4 (1990), 665–80.

Longman, Tremper, III. *How to Read the Psalms.* Downers Grove, IL: InterVarsity, 1988.

Marsh, John. *The Gospel of Saint John.* London: Penguin, 1968.

Marshall, Alfred. *The RSV Interlinear Greek-English New Testament.* London: Samuel Bagster and Sons, 1968.

Phillips, Elaine A. "The Pools of Siloam." *Tyndale Bulletin* 70.1 (2019) 41–54. doi:10.53751/001c.27711.

Rae, Murray. "To Render Praise: Humanity in God's World." In *The Doctrine of God and Theological Ethics*, edited by Allan J. Torrance and Michael Banner, 201–20. London: T&T Clark, 2006.

Taylor, Joan E. "Pontius Pilate and the Imperial Cult in Roman Judaea." *New Testament Studies* 52 (2006) 555–82. doi:10.1017/S0028688506000300.

Thurmer, John. *The Son in the Bible and the Church.* Exeter: Paternoster, 1987.

Verney, Stephen. *Water into Wine: An Introduction to John's Gospel.* London: Fount, 1985.

Wallace, David B. "The Gospel of John: Introduction, Argument, Outline." New Testament: Introductions and Outlines. Bible.org. https://bible.org/seriespage/gospel-john-introduction-argument-outline.

Wenham, David, and Steve Walton. *Exploring the New Testament: The Gospels and Acts.* Vol. 1. 2nd ed. London: SPCK, 2011.

Wright, Tom. *How God Became King.* London: SPCK, 2012.

———. *John for Everyone, Part 1.* London: SPCK, 2002.

———. *John for Everyone, Part 2.* London: SPCK, 2002.

Wright, N. T. *Jesus and the Victory of God.* London: SPCK, 1996.

Bibliography

———. *The New Testament and the People of God*. Minneapolis: Fortress, 1992.
———. *Paul and the Faithfulness of God*. London: SPCK, 2013.
———. *The Resurrection of the Son of God*. London: SPCK, 2003.
———. *Surprised by Scripture*. London: SPCK, 2014.
Wright, N. T., and Michael F. Bird. *The New Testament in Its World*. London: SPCK, 2019.

INDEX

Abraham, 62, 64, 88n6
Aenon near Salim, 38
Annas, 106, 122, 123, 129n21
apostles, 2, 3, 13n29, 42, 134

becoming, 27
believe, 8, 9, 12, 24, 30, 36, 37, 44, 52, 59, 60, 65, 72, 78–80, 82, 84, 88, 90, 93, 95, 100, 108, 110–12, 115, 119, 133, 137, 138
Bethany, 82, 85
Bethel, 24n21, 25
bios, 1
blood, 10, 35n6, 58, 129
bread, 12, 53, 55–59, 124, 140, 141

Caesar, 45, 125, 126
Caiaphas, 81, 82, 122
Cana, 13, 27, 95
Capernaum, 55–57
Cephas, see Simon Peter
command(s), commandment(s), 48, 99, 104n28, 105
Council, Jewish (Sanhedrin), 31, 32
creation, 9, 17, 18, 21, 26, 49, 56, 84, 135
crucifixion, 10, 37, 64, 89, 126, 128

death, 9, 11, 12, 30n15, 31, 46, 64, 82, 84, 85, 88–90, 94, 95, 97, 99, 100, 103, 110, 111, 127, 129, 131n1

direct parallel(ism), 5, 6, 14, 19, 34, 36, 37, 39, 43–44, 50, 52, 59, 77, 84, 90, 107

Ephraim, 3, 81
eternal life, 12, 21, 36, 37, 41, 43, 50, 57n10, 58, 59, 79, 84, 90, 112, 116
eucharist, see Lord's Supper
exodus, 53, 64, 93
eyewitness, 1, 4, 129, 132

Farewell Discourse, 13, 14, 92, 111, 115, 118, 136
Father, of Jesus, 18, 20, 21, 36, 48–52, 58, 60, 63–65, 70, 76–80, 90, 94, 96, 97, 99–102, 105, 107, 110n35, 111–19, 134, 138; of disciples, 19, 34, 109n34, 134
Festival, of Dedication of the Temple, 29, 77; of Shelters, xv, 29, 61–62, 72, 78
flesh, 12, 19, 27, 58
food, 12, 53, 54, 58

Gabbatha, 3
ginomai, 27
glory, glorify(ing), 9, 10, 19, 27, 37, 64, 88, 90, 93, 96, 97, 101–2, 110, 114–16, 119, 127
God's children, 19, 27, 139

Index

go(ing), 65, 94, 97, 99–101, 109n34, 110, 111
Greek(s), 17, 19, 77, 88–90

hatred, 93, 105–7
Heraclitus, 17
Herod (Antipas), 31, 51
high priest, 3, 81, 106, 116–17, 120, 122–24, 129n21
hina, 95, 105, 107, 111, 115, 118, 119
Holy Spirit, 20, 21, 34, 35n11, 38, 44, 60, 63n8, 98n10, 100, 102, 107, 109n34, 110, 118, 135
hour, 10, 90, 94, 127
hunger, hungry, 56, 59

"I am" sayings, 43; absolute, 43, 56, 62, 64, 66, 95, 96n6, 120–22; with predicates, 58–59, 63n8, 65, 75n4, 83n3, 84, 98n10, 101, 104
identity, of Jesus, 1, 17, 18, 21, 22, 36, 43, 46, 62, 64, 65, 72, 79, 89, 96, 120, 137; of gospel author, 2; of disciples, 21, 24, 72, 134
incarnation, 18–19, 61, 89n7, 94
Isaiah, 21, 43, 88
Israel, 20–22, 29, 33, 44, 56, 64, 65, 66, 72–76, 80n20, 90, 93, 103, 117

Jacob, 24n21, 41, 88n6
Jeremiah, 73
Jerusalem, 3, 4, 11, 26, 29, 30, 47, 62, 70, 77, 87, 88n3, 128
John, author, "the disciple Jesus loved," 2, 4, 132, 133, 141, 142
John, the Baptist, 16, 18, 19, 21, 22, 32, 37–39, 51, 88n6
John the Elder, 2–4
John, son of Zebedee, 2, 4, 140

Joseph of Arimathea, 130
joy, 62, 88n3, 93, 103, 105, 115, 118, 119, 134–36
Judas (not Iscariot), 97, 100, 102, 107
Judas Iscariot, 60, 86, 87, 96, 97
judge, judgment, 11, 12, 29, 31, 35, 50, 64, 67, 72n6, 90, 110, 125

King of Israel, 21, 22, 87, 88, 120, 127n15, 129, 130
Kingdom of God, 9, 29, 34, 37, 125, 126, 129n19
know(ing), 11, 20, 22, 33, 44, 59n12, 64, 65, 71, 76, 77, 99, 101, 107, 112, 114, 116, 119

Lamb of God, 22, 124, 127
Lazarus, 3, 9, 11, 46, 81–82, 85
light, 18, 35, 62, 63n8, 65, 66, 72, 81, 88, 90
logos, 17, 18, 50, 59
Lord's Supper, 12, 53, 55, 141
love, loving, xv, 19, 27n4, 35–37, 76, 79, 93, 98n10, 99, 101n17, 102, 103, 105, 111, 114, 117, 119, 141

Malchus, 3
Martha, 3, 82, 84
Mary of Bethany, sister of Martha and Lazarus, 3, 82, 84, 85–87
Mary of Magdala, 42, 132–34
Mary, mother of Jesus, 4, 10, 27
menein, 103n22
Messiah, 17, 20, 21, 23, 28, 43, 64–66, 73, 78, 82, 129
Moses, 12, 44, 52, 54, 58, 61, 64, 68, 69n30, 88n6
Mount Gerizim, 41, 43
Mount Zion, 43, 77

Naqdimon, see Nicodemus
Nathaniel, 22, 23, 139

Index

new creation, 9, 10, 26, 48, 84, 130, 132, 135
new exodus, 9, 30, 53, 55, 85, 130
Nicodemus, 3, 13, 32, 33, 41, 58, 66, 130

obey, obedience, 21, 28, 48, 64, 71, 79, 99, 102, 103, 105

paracletos, 98n10, 102n20
Papias of Hierapolis, 2
Passover, 26, 29, 30, 53, 85, 93, 127, 130; Passover lamb, 130
peace, 88, 109n34, 111, 126, 136
Peter, 24, 60, 95, 99, 121, 123, 132, 133, 140–42
Pharisee(s), 33
Philip, 24, 44, 97, 100, 101, 139
Philo, 18
pisteuein, 37
Plato, 18
poiein, 49
Pontius Pilate, 13, 120, 124–28
Pool of Bethzatha, 3, 9, 11, 47, 70
Pool of Siloam, 3, 9, 11, 61, 70, 77
prologue, 16, 18, 19, 27, 34, 49, 139
prophet, 43, 54, 73

remain, 103
resurrection, 10–12, 24, 31, 42, 48, 50, 59, 82, 84, 94, 100, 103, 111, 131, 133, 137, 138, 139
Roman, 81, 124, 138

Sabbath, 11, 64, 77, 130
sacrifice, 31, 58, 76, 77, 100, 105, 114, 124, 127, 129
salvation, 44, 65, 77, 143
Samaritan woman, 13, 40–43, 50, 56, 58
sarx, 19
savior, 9, 35, 44, 90

see(ing), 20, 34, 37, 42, 71, 72, 88–90, 101, 109n34, 111, 114, 119, 135–38
semeia, 8, 26
shalom, 64, 72, 136
sheep, 74–78
Sheep Gate, 3
Shema, 79
shepherd, 74 –77,
sign(s), 8–13, 26, 27, 31, 45, 46n12, 54, 58n10, 59, 72, 77, 131
Simon Peter, see Peter
sin, 9, 10, 22, 68, 69, 72, 95, 100, 107, 110, 129
Solomon's Portico, 3
Son of God, 20–22, 36, 79, 126
Son of Man, 36, 37, 72, 89
"so that" sayings, 92, 93, 95, 100, 105, 107, 108, 111, 119
Spirit of God, see Holy Spirit
Stoics, 18
Stone Pavement, 3
suffering, 84, 90, 103, 107, 111, 121
Synoptic Gospels, 3, 12, 21, 29, 99n12, 104n27, 139

temple, 26, 29, 30n15, 31, 44, 61, 62, 77, 85n1, 88n3, 124, 128, 131
third day, 10, 131n1
thirst(y), 41, 42, 59, 65, 129
Thomas, 97, 100, 135–138
titulus, 128
Torah, 18, 64, 69,
truth, 18, 27, 37, 39, 64–66, 98n10, 101, 102, 110, 119, 126

union, unity, 79, 93, 103–5, 113n39, 115, 116, 118, 119,

vine, 99, 103, 104n26

wadi Kidron, 3

Index

water, 9, 10, 22, 26, 29, 34, 35n6, 41–45, 62, 63n8, 65, 95, 129
water-pouring ceremony, 61, 65
wine, 9, 10, 26, 28, 29, 45, 141
woman charged with adultery, xv, 12, 63n8, 67–69
word, 17–19, 22, 27, 50

world, 9, 10, 12, 17, 21, 22, 27, 29, 33n5, 44, 48, 63n8, 65, 70, 72, 77, 79, 88–90, 93, 99, 102, 105–7, 110, 114, 115, 117–20, 125, 126, 129, 135, 136
worship, 43, 44, 61, 85n1, 122, 129n19, 135, 137

www.ingramcontent.com/pod-product-compliance
Lightning Source LLC
Chambersburg PA
CBHW072138160426
43197CB00012B/2151